Family Reset:
Building Eternal Bonds

Mariangeli Moruaske

COPYRIGHT © 2025 by Mariángeli Morauske.

Mariángeli Morauske, MD, MACP., MAPM., Ch., affirms the moral right to be identified as the author of this work.

Edited by Mariangeli Morauske and artificial intelligent.

Top image: Inteligencia Artificial It does not correspond to real people.

Printed in the United States of America. All rights reserved.
Imprint: Published independently.

No part of this book may be reproduced, stored in a retrieval system, or transmitted in any form or by any means, electronic, mechanical, photocopying, recording, scanning, or otherwise, without the prior written permission of the author, except for short quotations used in critical reviews or articles. Permission can be requested by contacting the author by email at endtimessequence@aol.com.

Unless otherwise indicated, all quotations from Sacred Scripture are taken from the 1960 King James Version.

Ellen G. White's quotes are from the online collection of her writings available on www.egwwritings.org. Copyright © 2025 by Ellen G. White Estate, Inc. Used with permission. All rights reserved.

ISBN: 979-8-89860-256-7 paperback

Family Reset: Building Eternal Bonds

Table of Contents

Dedication iii
Message to the Reader v

Chapter 1: The First Sanctuary...................................1
   Tools to transform your home 3

Chapter 2: When the Home Breaks Down 9
   Recognizing cracks as the beginning of restoration 13
   The Hidden Cracks No One Sees: Silent Signs of Family Disconnection... 19
   Five Steps to Restoring What Seems Lost: A Path to Healing 26
   Practical Tools for Restoring the Home: Cultivating Love, Unity, and Purpose 30
   Practical Steps to Home Restoration 33
   Start the Process: Building a Heaven in Your Home 35

Chapter 3: The Transforming Power of Time 39
   The Tragedy of Dead-End Absence: The Impact of Disconnection.. 49
   Tools to Transform the Home: Turning Time into Intentional Love... 52

Chapter 4: The Transforming Power of Love......... 57
   Characteristics of Transformative Love in Action 62
   Tools to rekindle love at home:............................. 64

Chapter 5: The Transformative Power of Communication 71
   Signs that communication is broken 73
   Tools to restore communication in your home .. 74

Family Reset: Building Eternal Bonds

Chapter 6: The Transforming Power of Prayer......77
 The Effect of Absence of Prayer in the Home 83
 Impacts of Praying in Unity 88
 Renovating the Family Altar Day by Day: Small Steps to Transform the Home. 94

Chapter 7: The Restoration of the Lost Sons 103
 Steps towards restoring bonds with your children 105
 Practical tools for parent advocates:.................109

Chapter 8: How to Forgive Without Losing Yourself 117
 Forgiveness According to Heaven....................117
 What does it mean to forgive without getting lost? 118
 Tools for Practicing Family Forgiveness............120
 The Healing Power of Forgiveness in the Home – Transforming the Home into a Sanctuary of Peace 120

Chapter 9: Traditions that Heal, and Unite 125
 How to create family traditions that unite and uplift? 131

Chapter 10: The Joy of Being a Purposeful Family 137
 God's Purpose for the Family............................137
 How to discover the purpose of our family? ...140
 Tools to build a family with a mission..............142

Chapter 11: From Ruins to Redemption 147
 Tools to build a home a Heavenly Home 149

Meet the Author..153
Bibliography..155

Family Reset:Building Eternal Bonds

Dedication

To my beloved husband Daniel, your love has been the most beautiful page in my history. In every chapter of my life, you are the main character, the one who inspires and strengthens me.

This book is dedicated to you, as a small reflection of the great mark you have left on my heart and spirit. Thank you for being my light, my unconditional support, and my greatest blessing. This journey, shared with you, makes every word more meaningful.

With all my love and gratitude.
Mariangeli

Family Reset:Building Eternal Bonds

Family Reset:Building Eternal Bonds
Message to the Reader

Dear reader,

This book is not just a set of chapters or a manual with isolated principles; It is a heartfelt invitation to begin a transformative journey, a journey toward building a home that is a true reflection of heaven on earth. It's more than words on paper, it's a living heartbeat that wants to resonate in your heart and that of your family, to inspire you to build relationships filled with love, purpose, and divine grace.

It's not just about giving you practical advice or structured tools. It is a personal, deep and intentional call for you to take a moment to reflect, to look into your soul and discover that purpose that God has designed specifically for your family. This book is full of tools to help you create a home where love is genuine, where forgiveness is the usual language, where prayer transforms the atmosphere, and where Jesus is not an occasional visitor, but a permanent inhabitant.

I invite you to read calmly, with an open heart and attentive eyes. Each chapter has been written to speak to your soul, ignite in your spirit the longing for meaningful change, and offer you clear principles that you can apply in your day-to-day life. This book is designed for you, for your family, for your friends, for those around you. Take the time to

Family Reset: Building Eternal Bonds

meditate, underline, write down your thoughts, and share what inspires you with those you love. These pages are not only intended to be a mirror for you to reflect on your family life, but also a bridge to get closer to the people with whom you share your life.

And if you decide to embark on this journey, you should know that you will not be alone. Each page has been created with love and purpose, to be your partner in this transformation. Every reflection is a whisper of hope, every principle is a seed of change. Read it on your own, with your partner, or in a family circle. Allow yourself the time to let every word resonate in your home, taking root in the depths of your relationships and laying the foundation for an everlasting legacy.

This book does not seek perfection in you or your family, because perfection is not the requirement for building a heavenly home. All you need is a willing heart, a living faith, and a sincere prayer that says, *"Lord, begin with me. Make my home a place where Your love, Your grace, and Your peace dwell."*

Today is the time to take that first step. Don't wait for a better day, don't look for a more suitable time. This book is not just another resource; It's a start. The beginning of a new story in your home. A story where love transcends words, where faith illuminates the darkest days and where hope becomes the force that unites your family.

Family Reset:Building Eternal Bonds

Do you dare to build a sky in your home? It all starts with you: with your faith on fire, with your willingness to live with purpose, and with your desire to build bonds that transcend time. Because when you decide to walk on this mission, you begin to sow seeds of heaven here on earth, transforming your home into a sanctuary of love and redemption.

With deep caring, hope, and gratitude, The Team Behind *A Heavenly Home: Building Eternal Bonds*

Each page was written recognizing that we are all on a path of learning and transformation. Therefore, I want to share with you this important notice:

Disclaimer: A Living and Evolving Book

1. Errors and corrections: This book has been written with dedication, honesty, and a deep desire to share truths that transform. However, I recognize that while I have made an effort to provide clear, truthful, and carefully edited content, you may encounter some errors. If this is the case, I thank you in advance for your patience and understanding, as such errors do not affect the essence or value of the book's message.

Your contribution is valuable and welcome. If you find anything that needs to be corrected, please email me at: **endtimessequence@aol.com**. I will be happy to correct it in future editions and, with your

Family Reset: Building Eternal Bonds

permission, give you credit for your help, which will contribute to the enrichment of the message of this work.

2. Progressive interpretation: It is important to note that my understanding of the content is progressive. I am constantly growing and open to understanding. Some ideas may evolve over time, as I receive more light, experience, or revelation. This book humbly reflects what I have learned, lived and understood so far. It is an honest testimony of my personal and spiritual journey, which will continue to unfold.

Thank you for being part of this living process. Your reading and application of the principles shared here are the true heart of this work, which seeks to inspire, heal, and build families to reflect heaven on earth. Your interaction and feedback are an essential part of this purpose.

Chapter 1: The First Sanctuary
The Family as a Reflection of Heaven

What if I told you that heaven doesn't start up there, but down here, in the place where you eat, laugh, cry, and love? The family is not just a group of people united by blood. It is the first sanctuary that God designed to reveal His character to the world. In the midst of modern chaos, homes must be transformed into temples of hope, where every heart beats in harmony with heaven.

When God created man and woman, He did not begin with a church, a school, or a nation, but with a home. Eden was the first human home, and in it, the family was established as the purest reflection of his image. Genesis 1:27 states, "And God created man in his own image, in the image of God he created him; male and female he created them."

The family is, therefore, the first mirror of heaven. It is not only about coexistence, but about eternal purpose.

"Every Christian family should illustrate to the world the power and excellence of Christian influence.... Parents should realize their accountability to keep their homes free from every taint of moral evil" (*The Adventist Home*. P. 19.5).

The restoration and upliftment of mankind begins with the home.

Family Reset: Building Eternal Bonds

The Power That Shapes Lives

Every word that is said at home, every look, every decision, contributes to the construction of the character of those who inhabit it. Therefore, it is no exaggeration to say that the future of humanity is forged in the privacy of homes. The home should be a school where God's children prepare for the mansion that Christ has gone to prepare for those who love Him. "The elevation or deterioration of the future of society will be determined by the manners and morals of the youth growing up around us. As the youth are educated, and as their characters are molded in their childhood to virtuous habits, self-control, and temperance, so will their influence be upon society" (*The Adventist Home*. p. 15.2),.

"Home should be made all that the word implies. It should be a little heaven upon earth, a place where the affections are cultivated instead of being studiously repressed. Our happiness depends upon this cultivation of love, sympathy, and true courtesy to one another" (*The Adventist Home*. p. 15.3).

Our homes are forming citizens of heaven or the world. Happy families are not born, they are built. They are sculpted with love, faith, sacrifice, and purpose. How much time do we dedicate to this sanctuary? Are we erecting altars of prayer or monuments of distraction?

Family Reset:Building Eternal Bonds

The first place in priorities

Jesus never said, "Seek first professional success," but rather, "Seek first the kingdom of God and his righteousness, and all these things will be added to you." (Matthew 6:33). If we want to build eternal bonds, we must start by placing our family at the center of our priorities.

Do an exercise: check your calendar for the past week. Where is your family in it? What percentage of your hours was invested in strengthening your most important relationships? What is not scheduled, is lost.

Tools to transform your home

Here is an expanded, deeper and enriched version of the tools to transform your home, with concrete examples and practical reflections:

1. **Sacred Dialogue: Opening the heart to connect deeply.** Sacred dialogue is more than a conversation: it is an act of love and self-giving. Set aside a specific time of day, without distractions, to talk to your family. This time should be free of phones, televisions, or other interruptions to allow for active and empathetic listening.

For example, before bedtime, gather in the living room or around the table to share something meaningful that happened to you during the day.

Family Reset:Building Eternal Bonds

Ask deep questions like, "What are you most grateful for today?" or "What time of day made you feel special?" As you listen, practice validating your feelings by saying things like, "I understand how that could be hard for you." This space will build trust and strengthen emotional bonds.

2. **The Family Altar: A Sacred Time of Spiritual Connection.** Restoring family worship does not require long hours. Spend just 10 minutes each day praying together, reading a Bible passage, or reflecting on a spiritual topic.

   An example might be choosing a verse each week, such as Psalm 133:1: "See how good and how pleasant it is for the brethren to dwell together in harmony!" Afterward, each member can share a personal reflection on how to apply it in their lives. Even the youngest can participate by drawing what they understood from the passage. This family altar not only binds the family together, but also renews its spiritual purpose.

3. **The Day of Blessing: Creating memories that transcend.** Dedicate one day a month to do something special as a family, creating an atmosphere of joy and unity. You don't need a

Family Reset:Building Eternal Bonds

big budget; the important thing is the intention and the connection.

For example, host a themed dinner at home, such as an "Italian night," where everyone helps make pizza from scratch. Alternatively, head out into the park with a blanket for a picnic, carrying a list of outdoor games and activities, such as flying a kite or playing family charades. These moments will become cherished memories and strengthen the bonds between you.

4. **The Family Gratitude List: Cultivating Grateful Hearts.** The habit of gratitude transforms perspectives and strengthens bonds. Each week, gather as a family and write down three blessings you have experienced together.

   For example, they could include moments like, "We all cooked together on Sunday," "We supported each other through a difficult time," or "We thanked God for the family's health." Place this list in a visible place, such as the refrigerator, and review it at the end of the month. Not only will this create a sense of gratitude, but it will also help them remember how much they have, so they feel blessed.

5. **The Priority Commitment: Building a Home Centered on Love.** This commitment is not only a statement, but a daily choice to show that home is the priority. This involves making intentional and practical decisions to put family first.

Family Reset:Building Eternal Bonds

For example, you can decide together to limit work hours after a certain time, prioritizing family dinner. You could also make an agreement to start each weekend with a family activity, such as a walk around the neighborhood or board game night. Be sure to regularly evaluate these priorities together, asking yourself, "What else can we do to make the home a haven of love and peace?"

Implementing these tools is an ongoing process that requires intention and dedication. Each is designed to cultivate unity, love, and spirituality in the home, making it a reflection of heaven.

Real-life example

I remember a mother who told me through tears, "I've worked all my life for my children, but I realize I was never really with them." Today, after losing her husband, she has turned her home into an anticipatory heaven, where her grandchildren find love, prayer, and purpose. She told me, "Now I understand that God gave me a second chance to build eternal bonds."

Your home is not a landform or an architectural structure. It is a living altar, a divine space to reflect God. The transformation will not come from outside or from empty promises. It begins with a decision: to make the home the place where heaven and earth embrace.

Family Reset:Building Eternal Bonds

For, in the words of Ellen G. White: The most important work that can be accomplished in this life is the work done in the home. "Fathers and mothers who make God first in their households, who teach their children that the fear of the Lord is the beginning of wisdom, glorify God before angels and before men by presenting to the world a well-ordered, well-disciplined family — a family that love and obey God instead of rebelling against Him" (*The Adventist Home*, p. 27.3).

Family Reset:Building Eternal Bonds

Family Reset:Building Eternal Bonds

Chapter 2: When the Home Breaks Down

Recognizing the Crisis and Restoring the Divine Blueprint

There are silences in homes that scream louder than words. There are dinners where the dishes sound louder than the voices. And there are beds that, even if shared by two people, are emptier than those in the desert. In my journey as a psychologist, I've found that many families break up long before anyone says it out loud.

But we were not born to live broken. Heaven was not designed to be a distant place that we arrive at only after we die, but a living reflection in the heart of every home. And when a family moves away from that design, sadness sets in, hope is extinguished... But a door is also opened: the door of restoration.

A reality that can no longer be denied

Marta came to my office with an envelope in her hand. It was his divorce summons. "I don't know how we got here," he said in a muffled voice. He was only forty years old, but his soul weighed on him like eighty. "I was happy. We had plans, we prayed together... At what point did it all fall apart?" What Marta didn't know was that she wasn't alone.

Family Reset:Building Eternal Bonds

More than half of families today live with broken ties, even though their social networks show otherwise. Children who grow up without affection, husbands who live together as strangers, mothers who love in solitude, and fathers who scream because no one taught them to cry.

The family, which should be the first place to breathe heaven, has been a constant target of an invisible enemy.

Satan is working with all power to destroy families. He knows that the heart of society, of the church, and of the nation is the home.

And if the enemy wants to destroy the home, it is because God's glory on earth begins there.

A reality that can no longer be denied: Stories that reflect broken hearts. Marta came to my office holding an envelope with trembling hands. It was his divorce summons. At just forty years old, his words revealed the weight of a worn soul: "I don't know how we got here. I was happy. We had plans, we prayed together... At what point did it all fall apart?" Marta didn't know it, but her story was shared by thousands of families who silently navigate waters of disconnection and pain.

This story is not an isolated case. **More than half of families today face broken ties**, although social networks tell a different narrative: smiling photos on vacation, optimistic posts of anniversaries, but a

Family Reset: Building Eternal Bonds

reality of silences, disconnection and wounded hearts behind the screen.

Case in point: Imagine a couple who post happy photos of a family vacation, but spend the entire trip arguing or isolated on their phones. This contrast between appearance and reality reflects a disconnect that needs to be addressed before the cracks turn into chasms.

The Family: Target of an Invisible Enemy. The home was designed by God as a refuge, the first place where you breathe heaven, but it has been constantly attacked by an invisible enemy. Satan is working with all power to destroy families. He knows that the heart of society, of the church, and of the nation is the home.

The enemy's attack is not always visible. It can manifest in unspoken words, absent hugs, or in the routine that slowly replaces intentional connection. Every unrestored criticism, every forgotten prayer, and every elusive glance becomes tools of the enemy to fragment the divine design of the home.

Reflection: If Satan fights so fiercely to destroy the home, it is because he understands his divine purpose. Every family is a potential reflection of God's glory on earth. Defending this space starts with being aware of its value and working daily to protect it.

Family Reset:Building Eternal Bonds

A divine design that can be restored. The home was not a human invention, but the first sanctuary created by God. Adam and Eve began their existence in a garden of love and fellowship, not in a stone temple. The first altar was an embrace, and the first prayer, a conversation between spouses who walked with God at sunset. Although sin disfigured this perfect design, God's purpose never changed.

Practical example: Think of a modern home that recaptures this divine simplicity. Something as simple as walking together after dinner or taking a few minutes to share how each of you experienced God's presence in your day can invite back the connection that Adam and Eve enjoyed.

Reflection: God still desires to sit at our tables, hear our laughter, and be the invisible link that strengthens our relationships. Let him be the architect of our families.

The pain behind the numbers: True stories that reflect cracks. Stories like Marta's are not unique. In homes all over the world, children grow up without the necessary affection, husbands live together as strangers, mothers love in solitude and fathers suppress their emotions in screams because they never learned to cry. These dynamics do not always

Family Reset: Building Eternal Bonds

result in visible divorces, but they do result in emotionally disconnected families.

Case in point: Martha could have avoided getting to the point of divorce if she and her husband had recognized the cracks in time. Something as simple as setting up a monthly night for deep conversations or seeking pastoral guidance can be the tipping point in repairing what seems hopeless.

Recognizing the Cracks as the Beginning of Restoration

Often, families don't need a public crisis to realize that something is wrong; it is enough to be silent and listen to what is not being said. That silence can be painful, but it's also the first step toward restoration. Cracks are not synonymous with defeat; they are opportunities to invite God to rebuild.

Practical example: Take a moment of evaluation as a family, saying, "What can we do to connect better? How can we bring God back to the center of our decisions?" These questions not only invite reflection, but open the door to change.

The family as a reflection of God's glory The enemy attacks the home because he knows that God's glory on earth begins there. Every act of love, every reconciliation, and every prayer in the family is a

Family Reset: Building Eternal Bonds

living testimony that heaven can be manifested in the home.

Practical example: What would happen if each family member made a personal commitment? "Today I will choose to affirm, instead of criticize"; "Today I will choose to listen, rather than react." These small gestures, when repeated daily, can turn a fractured home into a place of divine restoration. God is still writing resurrection stories in homes that choose to give themselves to Him.

A design that can still be restored

The home was the first sanctuary. Adam and Eve did not begin their existence in a stone temple, but in a garden of love, care, and fellowship. The first altar was a hug. The first prayer, a conversation between spouses who walked with God at sunset.

But from the entrance of sin, that design was disfigured. And yet, God's purpose never changed. God still wants to walk with us in the evening, to sit at our table, to be in the midst of our hugs and our decisions.

"If the Lord does not build the house, those who build it labor in vain; if the Lord does not guard the city, he keeps watch in vain." (Psalm 127:1)

Family Reset:Building Eternal Bonds

God wants to be the architect of our homes again. And that starts with recognizing the cracks.

The hidden cracks that no one sees: Some families don't scream.

The Hidden Cracks No One Sees: Signs of a Home in Need of Healing. Some families do not shout or have obvious conflicts. Its disconnection is not noisy, but it is installed silently, like a light that flashes until it is completely turned off. These cracks are invisible to those who observe from the outside, but deeply significant to those who experience them. The problem is not always a public crisis or a dramatic event; Sometimes the largest fractures are the quietest. Here are some signs that a home needs restoration:

1. When communication is reduced to the bare minimum.

Words in the home become functional tools rather than emotional bridges. Conversations are limited to what is necessary: "What time are you coming back?" "Did you pay the bills?" Communication does not flow as a channel of affection, but as a routine exchange that lacks depth.

Practical example: Imagine a family where the father and mother only talk about household chores or pending bills. One way to reactivate communication is to establish a weekly "connection

Family Reset:Building Eternal Bonds

hour", where everyone shares something personal: a dream, a challenge or even a happy memory. This reinvigorates dialogue and fosters a safe space to express emotions.

2. When family prayer is a blurred memory.

Prayer, that altar that unites families with God, becomes something relegated to the past. The routine of seeking divine direction together disappears, leaving the home without a spiritual compass. A home that is no longer united is more vulnerable to disconnection.

Practical example: Dedicate five minutes a day to begin or end together in prayer. If the family is not yet willing, start only as an intercessor and ask God to touch the hearts of others. Once prayer is resumed as a habit, the home will begin to regain its spiritual strength.

3. When the eyes no longer meet, they are only avoided.

Eye contact, which was once a natural gesture full of love and connection, disappears. Instead, glances are dodged, reflecting emotional distance and unresolved conflicts. This change happens gradually and often goes unnoticed until the distance becomes profound.

Practical example: Do family activities that require visual interaction, such as a game in which each

Family Reset:Building Eternal Bonds

member looks at another and shares something they admire about him or her. This simple act can rebuild trust and closeness between members.

4. When children prefer the street or the screen to the warmth of the home.

Children and adolescents look outside for what they do not find inside: acceptance, fun, connection. The house is no longer a refuge for them, but another place where they feel ignored or misunderstood. Screens or friends on the street become substitutes for family attention and affection.

Practical example: Designate a weekly "tech-free day" for meaningful family activities, such as cooking together, crafting, reading a book aloud, or playing outside. This shared time helps them to rediscover the richness of family life.

5. When there is more criticism than words of affirmation.

The home environment is filled with judgment and reproach, while words of encouragement, gratitude, and affirmation are relegated. Not only does this hurt family members, but it also weakens bonds, creating a cycle of disapproval that is difficult to break.

Practical example: Implement a family rule for each day: for every criticism made, at least three words of affirmation should be said. For example, instead of

Family Reset:Building Eternal Bonds

"You're always late," say, "I'm thankful you came. How can we better organize our time for the next one?"

6. The weight of silence: Listening to what is not said.

You don't need a big meltdown to know something is wrong. Sometimes, you just need to be quiet and pay attention. In that silence, unspoken truths emerge, repressed longings and wounds that have been covered with routine.

Practical example: Do a reflection exercise as a family. Sit in a circle together and ask each member to write on a piece of paper what you feel is missing in the home. Then, share these ideas without interrupting or judging. This act can be a catalyst for heartfelt conversations and meaningful change.

Recognizing Cracks as an Act of Courage

Recognizing cracks in the home is not a failure; it is the first step towards restoration. Disconnection doesn't have to be permanent. God can repair what is broken, heal the deepest wounds and restore light where today there are only blinks. By identifying these signs and acting with intention, any home can once again be a space of love, connection, and eternal purpose.

Family Reset:Building Eternal Bonds

The Hidden Cracks No One Sees: Silent Signs of Family Disconnection

In many homes, the cracks do not manifest themselves with open arguments or obvious conflicts; they are silent, invisible to others, but devastating to those who experience them. It is like a lamp whose light weakens over time until it is completely extinguished. These cracks often go unnoticed because they are not always accompanied by major crises, but their effects are deep and long-lasting.

Here are some signs that a home needs healing:

1. **Minimal communication:** Conversations are no longer deep or meaningful; they are limited to the practical and functional. Phrases such as "What time are you coming?" or "Did you pay the bill?" replace conversations about dreams, emotions or reflections. This creates an emotional void that slowly disconnects family members.

Practical example: One way to combat this is to implement a weekly "talk time," where each family member shares something personal: a dream, a challenge, or something that made them happy during the day. This space creates a bridge to recover lost communication.

2. **Forgotten Family Prayer:** What was once a natural, everyday act becomes a distant

Family Reset:Building Eternal Bonds

memory. The family no longer prays together or seeks God's guidance in their decisions. Without prayer, home loses its spiritual connection, leaving it vulnerable to discouragement and disconnection.

Practical example: Start small: pray together during meals or before bed. These simple actions can renew the spiritual habit in the home.

3. **Avoided glances:** Eyes that were once sought with love are now avoided. This doesn't happen overnight, but is the result of unresolved conflicts, accumulated resentments, or simply a lack of time together. The absence of eye contact is a reflection of emotional disconnection.

Practical example: A simple but powerful dynamic involves playing familiar games that involve direct interaction, such as looking into each other's eyes as they share a story or expressing something they are grateful for in each other.

4. **Disconnected children** : Children and adolescents, not finding affection or connection at home, seek refuge on screens or in the street. Gradually, their hearts drift apart, and home is no longer a safe place for them.

Practical example: Create a "tech-free day" where the whole family engages in meaningful activities together: cooking, crafting, walking outdoors, or just

Family Reset:Building Eternal Bonds

chatting. This dedicated time can restore a sense of connection in children.

5. **Words of criticism outweigh those of affirmation:**
   Instead of acknowledging efforts and virtues, family members focus on pointing out mistakes and defects. This creates an environment of tension where self-esteem wears out and love feels conditioned.

Practical example: Make a family commitment to replace each criticism with three words of affirmation. For example, instead of saying, "You never do anything right," try, "I really appreciate your effort; I know you can get better at this."

The Weight of Silence: Listening to What Is Not Said

Sometimes, you don't have to wait for a public crisis to realize something is wrong. It is enough to be silent. In that silence, you hear the unspoken words, the sighs that reflect a weight on the soul and the emotions that have been hidden for years.

Practical example: Propose an exercise of "reflective silence" as a family. Get together in a quiet space and spend five minutes writing down on paper how you feel and what you need from home. Then, share those notes. This activity can open the door to

Family Reset:Building Eternal Bonds

necessary conversations and be the first step to healing what is broken.

Restoring a Divine Design

Each of these hidden cracks is an opportunity to invite God to restore the original design of the home. He wants to be the center of our relationships, the point of union between each member of the family. No matter how dim the light in your home is, it can always be turned back on with love, intention, and faith.

A home that recognizes its cracks is not defeated; He is in the process of being redeemed. Let us open our lives to God so that, as the heavenly architect, he can transform our weaknesses into strengths and our cracks into bridges of love and eternal communion.

A story of resurrection

Gabriel and Mariana had been married for fifteen years. They seemed to have everything: a house, a car, a stable job, two children in Christian schools. But what they didn't have was peace. They slept in separate rooms. They prayed at different times. His children knew about it, but no one talked about it.

One day, her youngest son wrote on a school assignment: "My dream is that my parents love each

Family Reset:Building Eternal Bonds

other again." It was like a slap in the face from heaven. Mariana cried all night. Gabriel heard her and entered the room. They didn't talk much. They just held hands and prayed together for the first time in five years.

Today they are not perfect, but they have loved again. Because when God is invited to the center, the desert blooms.

A Resurrection Story: When the Desert Blooms

Gabriel and Mariana had been married for fifteen years. Apparently, they had everything: a comfortable house, cars, job stability and two children studying in Christian schools. Behind that image of success and normalcy, however, her home lacked something essential: peace. They slept in separate rooms, and although they continued to pray, they did so at different times, avoiding sharing that sacred space of communion. Her children sensed this disconnect, but no one talked about it; Silence had become the norm.

The Slap of the Sky: When the cracks come to light.

One day, her youngest son was given the task of writing about his biggest dream. Without filters or

Family Reset:Building Eternal Bonds

embellishments, she wrote: "*My dream is that my parents love each other again.*" This simple, but heartbreaking statement was like a slap from heaven for Mariana. That night, she cried inconsolably, facing the reality she had tried to ignore for so long. In the midst of his crying, Gabriel, who was listening from a distance, decided to enter the room. They didn't talk much, but, in a symbolic and powerful act, they held hands and prayed together for the first time in five years. From that moment on, something began to change.

Thoughtful example: Think about how many homes experience similar stories where the cracks remain hidden until someone—a child, a parent, a friend—shines a light on them. Sometimes, it's an unexpected comment, a sincere gesture, or even a shared dream, that triggers the restoration process.

The Transformation: Inviting God to the Center

Today, Gabriel and Mariana are not perfect; They still face challenges, but they have learned to walk together again. The peace they longed for did not come as a result of solving all their problems right away, but of inviting God into the center of their lives and their home. That act of humility and faith allowed her emotional wilderness to begin to blossom.

Family Reset:Building Eternal Bonds

Practical example: Gabriel and Mariana now dedicate one day a week to pray together as a couple. Each night before bed, they share a verse and a brief reflection on how to apply it in their family. These gestures don't take a lot of time, but they have a profound impact on your emotional and spiritual connection.

Lessons for Other Households: The Power of Small Gestures

This story is not only an inspiration to those facing fractured marriages; It's also a reminder that restoration starts with small but meaningful steps. Holding hands, sharing a prayer, or simply acknowledging that there are cracks, can change the dynamics of a home.

Practical example: For those who feel disconnected in their marriage, a good place to start may be to write a list of three things they admire about each other. Then, share it in a quiet environment, accompanied by a prayer. This act of affirmation can be the beginning of more honest and loving communication.

When God is invited, the desert blooms

Family Reset:Building Eternal Bonds

Gabriel and Mariana's story is a testament to the power of faith and humility. Even in the darkest of times, when separation seems inevitable, the act of inviting God into the center can transform hearts and relationships. God does not require perfection; He seeks willingness and dedication, and it is in that space where he works miracles.

Final Thought: When families acknowledge their wounds and allow God to be the healer, the cracks become points of restoration, and the home a reflection of His glory.

Five Steps to Restoring What Seems Lost: A Path to Healing

Restoring a home is not an instantaneous process, but with faith, intention, and concrete actions, what seems lost can come back to life. Each step is a stepping stone to a renovated, purpose-filled home. Here we break them down in depth:

1. Recognize without guilt: Accepting the crisis as a starting point.

Accepting that there is a crisis is not a sign of failure, but an act of courage. Recognizing the cracks in the home without blaming yourself or others is critical to starting the path to healing. This attitude does not seek to define culprits, but to find solutions.

Family Reset:Building Eternal Bonds

Reflective example: Think of a family that faces constant tensions between parents and children. By recognizing that there is a problem, it opens the door to dialogue. A parent may say, "I know we've been distant lately. I want to find a way to reconnect with you." This small act of humility and sincerity can disarm the initial tension.

2. Stop and observe: Rediscovering home with intention.

In a world full of distractions, stopping to observe is an act of reconnection. Do a "spiritual retreat" within your own home. Turn off screens, leave pending tasks and dedicate exclusive time to observe. Look at yourself. Look at them. Listen to what is not said, the gestures, the looks.

Practical example: Dedicate an afternoon to sit in the center of the home with your family in silence. Ask questions like, "How has our home been feeling lately?" or "What can we do to be more united?" This exercise reveals hidden dynamics and opens space for deep dialogue.

3. Restoring the altar: Regaining spiritual strength.

Family Reset:Building Eternal Bonds

There is no strong family, without prayer. Even if you're the only one just starting out, your intercession can be the starting point for home restoration. In the Bible, we see how God responds when a heart humbles itself and cries out for direction. The restoration of the altar is not only a spiritual act, it is a symbol that the home puts God back at the center.

Practical example: Make a commitment to pray every night as a family, even if it's only for five minutes. You can start with something simple, such as giving thanks for three blessings of the day or reading a Bible verse together. Over time, this act can transform the spiritual environment of the home.

4. Seek spiritual and professional help: New paths through guidance and wisdom.

Sometimes, the solution is not only in our hands. Seeking help is not a sign of weakness, but of wisdom. God can use pastors, therapists, books, or even a conversation with someone wise to open up new perspectives and opportunities for change.

Practical example: A couple facing marital difficulties could attend pastoral or family counseling sessions. In the meantime, children can find support in a trusted mentor. The combination

Family Reset: Building Eternal Bonds

of spiritual and professional guidance acts as a compass to restore what seems lost.

5. Forgiving to Live: Healing Through Forgiveness

Forgiveness is not forgetting, but renouncing the right to continue bleeding from a wound. It is a liberating act, both for the giver and for the receiver. Jesus taught us to forgive not only as an act of compassion, but as a doorway to true freedom.

Reflective example: Imagine a father who has been distant with his son. A simple: "I'm sorry for not being there as I should have been. I want to do better" can become a turning point. Forgiveness rebuilds bridges where there were only ruins.

One step at a time towards restoration

Each of these five steps not only addresses the visible part of the problem, but delves into the roots of family disconnection. Acknowledging, observing, praying, seeking help, and forgiving are everyday acts that, over time, can transform what seems lost into a story of resurrection and hope.

God is always willing to restore homes that are opened to His guidance. It just needs a heart willing to take the first step.

Family Reset: Building Eternal Bonds

Practical Tools for Restoring the Home: Cultivating Love, Unity, and Purpose

These tools are designed to help you rekindle family bonds, heal wounds, and bring God into the center of the home. Each offers simple, yet transformative steps that, when practiced with intention, can turn your home into a space of eternal love and purpose.

✤ Home Diagnosis: Listening to and Understanding Hearts at Home

The "Home Diagnosis" is a tool to stop and analyze how each member of the family feels in the space they share. Ask questions like, "Do I feel heard?" "Do I feel like I'm loved here?" and "What would I change?" allows each voice to be heard without judgment, revealing areas that need attention.

Practical example: On a quiet afternoon, gather your family in a circle. Each member writes their answers on sheets of paper that are then read aloud. Not only will this help identify cracks, but it will also foster empathy. For example, if a child says, "I feel like no one is listening to me when I speak," that can open the door to conversations and commitments to change.

Reflection: Responses are not critical, but opportunities to improve together. This act shows each family member that their feelings matter.

Family Reset: Building Eternal Bonds

📖 Restoration Journal: Crying Out to Heaven Through Daily Prayer

Constant prayer is a powerful tool of restoration. Writing a daily prayer for your home, your children, your marriage, or your own struggles allows you to create a space for communication with God and personal reflection. Over time, you will notice how your cry touches the sky and transforms hearts.

Practical example: Spend five minutes each morning or evening writing a sentence in a special notebook. You can include gratitude, petitions, and words of faith. For example: "Lord, lead my home to unity, teach us to forgive each other and be a reflection of Your love." At the end of the month, review your prayers and notice the answers God has begun to manifest.

Reflection: This journal is not only a record of your spiritual journey, but a testimony of how God works in perfect timing.

🏆 Circle of Gratitude: Cultivating Love with Words

Love is not required; it is cultivated through actions and words that nourish. The Gratitude Circle is a ritual where, every Friday during dinner, each member says something they are grateful for from

Family Reset: Building Eternal Bonds

the others. This exercise creates an environment of affirmation and mutual appreciation.

Practical example: Before serving the meal, invite each member of the family to share something positive. For example, a parent might say, "I thank Mom for always making us delicious dinners, even when she's tired." A child might add, "Thank you Dad for teaching me how to solve the math problem this week." These words build an environment where love and respect flourish.

Reflection: Gratitude transforms hearts and strengthens bonds, turning the everyday into extraordinary.

Day of Atonement: Healing Through Reconciliation

The Day of Atonement is a space dedicated to releasing emotional burdens and healing relationships. Choose a day of the month for each member to write letters (they can be symbolic) forgiving and asking for forgiveness. Then, as a family, pray together to give these wounds to God.

Practical example: Prepare a calm environment with soft music and lit candles. Each member writes his letter silently. An example might be: "I forgive my brother for not having supported me when I needed it, and I apologize for having reacted angrily." Once

Family Reset:Building Eternal Bonds

finished, keep them in a special place or burn them symbolically as an act of liberating the past.

Reflection: Forgiveness not only heals relationships, but also frees hearts from unnecessary burdens, allowing divine peace to fill the home.

Practical Steps to Home Restoration

These practical tools are not only symbolic acts; They are tangible ways to sow love, gratitude, and reconciliation in the home. With faith and intention, each family can experience how these small gestures transform their environment into one filled with peace and eternal purpose.

A Promise for Your Home: Restoring What Seemed Lost

"I will restore to you the years that the caterpillar, the leaping, the revolt, and the locust, my great army that I sent against you, ate." (Joel 2:25)

What a deep hope this promise holds! Not only does God have the power to heal what is happening in the present, but He can also redeem what the past has destroyed. The years consumed by pain, separation, or indifference are not wasted in His hands. What the enemy razed away, the Creator can rebuild with even greater glory. No matter how

Family Reset: Building Eternal Bonds

devastated the land of your home is, God has the ability to restore it and make it flourish again.

Thoughtful example: A family that has gone through a divorce may think that their story has come to a tragic end. However, by inviting God into their lives, lost love can be redeemed through new connections, emotional healing, and building relationships that reflect His grace.

Jesus at the Door: The Invitation to the Miracle

The promise does not end in the redeemed past; God also wants to transform your present. If your home today feels like a battlefield where relationships are broken or an empty room where loneliness reigns, you don't have to resign yourself. Jesus was at the door, knocking. He is not calling the church or the institutions. It's calling specifically to your home.

Case in point: Imagine a family reuniting after years of estrangement. A lonely mother, an estranged father, children who barely speak to each other. Through joint prayer and the humility of opening up to change, that home can be transformed into a space where grace and divine love are palpable. The key is to listen to that touch and respond with faith.

"I will save your children" (Isaiah 49:25) is a personal and powerful promise. No matter how far away your children may se—emotionally or spiritually—God—God ensures that His hand can reach them. Write this promise, pray with it, and

Family Reset: Building Eternal Bonds

repeat it in faith as a constant reminder that the battle for your home is not lost.

Start the Process: Building a Heaven in Your Home

Restoring a home doesn't happen overnight. It's a journey that requires patience, intention, and constant love. Every small step you take will be a seed that will eventually bear eternal fruit. Here are the fundamental pillars to start this process:

1. Recognizing the Need for Change: An Act of Humility and Hope

The first step in transforming a home is to recognize that something needs to change. This is not a sign of failure, but of courage. It is not about looking for blame or pointing out mistakes, but about surrendering your home to God, allowing Him to work on each member of the family and on the dynamics that need to be renewed.

Practical example: Gather your family in an honest conversation and say, "I feel like we've been disconnected. What can we do together to be more united?" This moment of reflection opens the doors for each member to share their thoughts and feelings, initiating the process of restoration.

Family Reset:Building Eternal Bonds

2. Gather Your Family in Prayer: The Altar That Unites Hearts

Prayer is the foundation for restoring any home. Even if it's just you at first, become an intercessor who prays fervently for your family's transformation. Constant prayer invites God to be the center of the home and acts as a spiritual glue that binds hearts together.

Practical example: Spend five minutes a day praying for your home. You can start by saying alone, "Lord, transform this home into a reflection of your love." Bless each member and lead us to unity." When others join in, incorporate moments of group prayer before meals or before bed. This habit, although simple, can transform the emotional and spiritual environment of the family.

3. Speak words of life: Sow affirmation instead of criticism

The words we use have a direct impact on relationships. It trades criticism and judgment for affirmations, gratitude, and hope. Every positive word you share is a seed that can blossom into love and trust in one another. A home where the words of life are the foundation is a home that breathes peace.

Family Reset:Building Eternal Bonds

Practical example: Make a commitment to practice daily affirmation. For example, instead of saying, "You never do things right," try saying, "I appreciate you trying, and I know you can do it." These small modifications can change the tone of interactions and strengthen family bonds.

4. Persevere in the process: Perseverance that bears eternal fruit

There will be difficult days where it will seem that things are not moving forward, but every tear shed, every act of love, and every prayer is part of building a heaven in your home. Restoration requires perseverance, and while the results may not be immediate, the process itself is valuable.

Practical example: Create a restoration journal where you record every little progress in your home. Write down how God has answered your prayers or how family interactions have changed. This record will not only motivate you, but it will also serve as a living testimony to the transformation that is occurring.

A path to restoration

Building a heaven in your home starts with small steps, but those steps have the power to completely

Family Reset: Building Eternal Bonds

transform the family environment. Recognizing the need for change, praying fervently, speaking words of life, and persevering are all practical tools that will help you create a home filled with love, purpose, and faith. No matter how broken the bonds may seem, God has the power to restore them and turn your home into a space where His glory shines.

Practical example: A family can set aside one day a week as a "day of restoration," where they read a Bible promise together and share how they can apply it in their daily lives. This time together becomes a pillar to strengthen family ties.

A Living Promise for Your Home

God's promise is not an abstract idea; It is a living reality that can manifest in your home if you choose to believe and act. Although today you may feel that the ruins are too big, remember that God specializes in rebuilding the impossible. There is still a table for you and your family in heaven, and God wants to start preparing it from your home.

Jesus is knocking on the door of your home, not as a judge, but as a restorer who brings with him peace, love, and hope. Invite Him in, trust His promise, and begin the process of redeeming what seemed lost today. With tears, love, and prayer, you can raise a heaven in your home.

Family Reset: Building Eternal Bonds

Chapter 3: The Transforming Power of Time
Sowing Eternity in the Minutes of the Present

The Measure of Love: Dedicating Time to the Eternal

"Tell me what you spend your time on and I'll tell you who you love." This phrase echoed in my childhood, but it wasn't until years later, after hearing stories of single mothers, wounded children, and distant husbands, that I understood its depth. Today I know that time is not only spent; it is invested or lost, and the most sacred thing is not the things we own, but those to whom we decide to give those precious minutes.

In this chapter, I want to invite you to see time with the eyes of heaven. If you want to build eternal bonds, you must sow **real presence** in the field of daily minutes. It is in those small acts of dedication where the bonds that transcend are built.

Time: The Measure of Love

I remember the story of Raúl, a successful man who came to my office. He had everything many would consider necessary to be happy: financial stability, professional achievements, and social recognition.

Family Reset:Building Eternal Bonds

But deep down, he was a broken man. He cried like a child, not because he lacked something material, but because he had too many absences. His words still shake me:

"I worked so that my family did not lack anything... but they lacked me."

Raul had spent his time on good things, but realized too late that he had neglected the most important thing: **his presence in the home**. In his attempt to provide, he forgot that love is not measured by the goods we give, but by the time we spend.

Thoughtful example: Imagine a parent who comes home from a long day at work and instead of sitting in front of the TV, spends 15 minutes playing with their children or listening to how their day went. That gesture, although simple, can transform the family dynamic and leave an indelible mark on their hearts.

Involuntary abandonment: When time is wasted unintentionally.

Many homes do not collapse because of hatred or open conflicts, but because of **involuntary abandonment**, because they do not understand that love is spelled with time. Without daily encounters, bonds weaken and eventually break. God did not ask us to build castles to impress the world, but

Family Reset:Building Eternal Bonds

family altars that reflect His presence. And altars are not raised in haste, but with pause, tenderness and dedication.

Spiritual Reflection: Ellen G. White wisely expressed: "Our work for Christ is to begin with the family, in the home.... There is no missionary field more important than this...." (*The Adventist Home*, p. 35.3).

, translated from the spanish version). But a well-ordered home is not limited to physical cleanliness; It is a space where time is given as a living offering, and where every act is guided by love.

Practical example: Dedicate one day a week as the "family altar day". Turn off your phones, prepare a special meal, and take time to pray, talk, and enjoy together without distractions. This quality time strengthens bonds and recalibrates the purpose of the home.

The Sowing of Time: Cultivating Eternal Bonds.

To build bonds that transcend, we must sow intentional time. This means being truly present, not only physically, but emotionally and spiritually. Every minute we dedicate to our family is like a seed that, with love and care, will germinate into strong and meaningful relationships.

Family Reset:Building Eternal Bonds

Thoughtful example: A mother can spend 20 minutes each night reading a bedtime story to her children. Although the act may seem small, it is in those shared moments that children feel loved and heard. These daily encounters build memories that become an eternal legacy.

Redeeming time, honoring love

Time is the most real measure of love. Not what we say, but what we do and how we choose to spend our minutes, reveals what we truly value. If today you feel that you have wasted time at home, do not be discouraged. God is a specialist in redeeming years that seemed lost.

Let us dedicate time to building family altars, to listening, to love without haste. Because, in the end, a well-ordered home is not the one that impresses the eyes of the world, but the one that gives every second as a living offering of love.

Final Thought: What can you do today to plant more time in your home? Even a small change in routine can make all the difference. Every moment invested in love is a treasure that neither time nor circumstances can erase.

The Divine Model of Time-Sharing

Family Reset: Building Eternal Bonds

From the beginning, God not only created life, but also created **the rhythm of time**. Six days of work... and one to meet us.

"And God finished on the seventh day the work which he made; and rested on the seventh day from all the work which he made." (Genesis 2:2)

God, who does not tire, set aside a day to show that the most important thing is not to produce, but to share.

Jesus also lived with this principle. In the midst of healings and crowds, He stopped. He went to the house of Lazarus, sat with the disciples, walked by the sea, talked at length with his disciples. I was never too busy to love.

Where Does Our Time Go?: An Honest Look at Our Priorities

It is common to hear the phrase: "*I don't have time!*" But is that really true? Often, lack of time is nothing more than a perception that hides a deeper truth: it is not a question of quantity, but of priorities. Our time is our most valuable resource, and how we use it reveals the priorities and values of our heart. As Scripture says, "For where your treasure is, there your heart will be also. (Matthew 6:21).

Family Reset:Building Eternal Bonds

If you want to know what you're investing your love and purpose in, start by looking at how you allocate your time. I invite you to do this exercise:

Make a weekly map of your hours: A diagnosis of your time.

Reflect honestly and answer:

- How many hours do you spend at work?
- How many hours do you spend on social media?
- How much time do you spend with your cell phone in your hand?
- And how many hours do you spend with your spouse or children, giving them your full attention?

Practical example: Take a notebook and draw a weekly schedule. Assign a color for each activity: work, social media play, cell phone use, family time, etc. At the end of the week, notice how your hours were distributed. You'll likely find that a lot of time is wasted on activities that don't bring eternal value, while the most important relationships are left behind.

The problem is not time, it is the priority

This exercise reveals an essential truth: it's not that you don't have time; it's that your priorities are defining how you use it. If you spend more hours on

Family Reset:Building Eternal Bonds

your cell phone than on your family, that's a reflection of what, in practice, comes first in your life. It doesn't matter how good your intention is if it's not backed up by concrete actions.

Thoughtful example: Imagine a parent who spends more than three hours a day on the cell phone, but only spends a few minutes talking to their children. Rearranging those priorities can make a monumental difference. Deciding to turn off your cell phone during dinner and talk as a family can transform a routine into a meaningful moment of connection.

Your time is your treasure: To whom do you give it?

Jesus taught us that where our treasure is, there our heart will be also. Time is one of our most precious treasures, and giving it to others is a tangible way to show love. It is not necessary to make great sacrifices; Dedicating small, but meaningful moments can change the dynamics of a home.

Practical example: Make a daily commitment to disconnect from screens for 30 minutes and dedicate that time exclusively to your children or spouse. You can use it to play games, read together, or just talk. This gesture not only strengthens family bonds, but also sends a powerful message: "You are more important than anything else."

Family Reset: Building Eternal Bonds

Building Eternal Bonds Through Time: The Investment That Transforms Lives

The time we spend with those we love is not just a resource; It is a seed that, when sown with intention, bears eternal fruit. Every hour and every minute we give with mindfulness becomes an act of love that transcends the present. Redirecting your time toward what really matters not only transforms your family relationships, but also strengthens your spiritual purpose, creating bonds that reflect divine grace.

The Sowing of Time: Small Gestures, Eternal Fruits

Building eternal bonds does not require drastic changes from one day to the next; it is achieved with small adjustments that, when accumulated, generate a significant transformation. The key is in the consistency and intention behind each act.

Practical example:

- Get up 15 minutes earlier to pray with your family before the day begins. This time not only connects the family spiritually, but also strengthens the relationship between its members.
- Set aside Fridays as "family night," where you tune out of screens to dine together, play board

Family Reset:Building Eternal Bonds

games, or just chat. These moments strengthen emotional bonds and create lasting memories.
- On your break from work, send a message of gratitude to a loved one. Something as simple as, "Thank you for your patience with me yesterday, it meant a lot to me," can change the tone of a relationship and reflect intentional love.

These small gestures sown daily have the power to build a heaven in your home, where love and connection are cultivated with dedication.

Prioritize what matters: Time as a reflection of the heart

We often say, "I don't have time," but in reality, the problem is not the lack of hours, but how we choose to use them. Time cannot be recovered, but it can be redirected. If you feel that a large part of your days have been dedicated to the urgent and you have put aside the important, today is the perfect time to make adjustments that reflect your true values.

Reflective example: Imagine that at the end of each week you review how you have used your time. How many hours did you spend on social media or work? And how many hours did you spend being fully present with your family? If the balance doesn't reflect your priorities, make small changes to correct it. For example, instead of watching TV after work,

Family Reset:Building Eternal Bonds

spend that time playing with your kids or having a meaningful conversation with your spouse.

Transformation: Time as an act of love

By giving your time to those you love, you are building bridges of love that will transcend the rush of daily life. Every moment spent with your loved ones is an eternal investment, a tangible reflection of the love God teaches us. Prioritizing your family and redirecting your time to them not only transforms the home; It also aligns your purpose with God's design.

Pause and ask yourself:

- How can I use my time to honor God?
- How can I show my family that they are my priority?

Answering these questions can be the beginning of a profound transformation in your routine, your home, and your heart.

A Life Focused on the Eternal

The time you have is a gift that you can't get back, but you can redirect it to what really matters. With small daily adjustments, you can transform your relationships, your purpose, and your home, building bonds that reflect God's eternal love. Remember that by giving your time as a living

Family Reset:Building Eternal Bonds

offering, you are sowing seeds that will blossom in the hearts of those you love most.

The Tragedy of Dead-End Absence: The Impact of Disconnection

Samuel was just 10 years old when he wrote a secret letter to God. In it, she expressed her deepest desire: *"I would like my dad to be like the ones in the movies. That he looked at me when I talked. To play with me."* His father, immersed in long working days, accidentally found that letter. As he read it, his son's words broke his heart. With tears in his eyes, he confessed to me: *"I've been so busy building the future that I'm missing the present... and my son."*

This revelation was the turning point in his life. She decided to make concrete changes to repair the relationship with her son: she started arriving early once a week, then twice. He turned off his cell phone during dinner and dedicated exclusive time to listen and play with Samuel. Over time, he became the father his son had always dreamed of. One day, Samuel wrote another letter, this time out loud: *"Thank you, God."* You gave me my dad back."

Time transforms when it is present

Family Reset:Building Eternal Bonds

You don't need perfect hours or ideal scenarios to transform your relationships. What you need are **sacred moments**, those moments when your children, your spouse, or your parents know that you are fully present and that you would not trade that moment for anything. In those moments, love becomes a tangible and transforming offering.

Case in point: Imagine a parent who sets aside 30 minutes each day to play with their children after work. Although it may seem like a small gesture, for children, that time translates into mindfulness, emotional validation, and a bond that grows stronger with each encounter.

The Impact of Time on Children and Teens

Studies confirm what the Bible already taught: Spending meaningful time with children has profound benefits. Children and adolescents who enjoy regular moments with their parents develop higher self-esteem, less tendency to addictions and healthier relationships. This time does not need to be elaborate or expensive; The most important thing is the intention and the quality of the presence.

Case in point: A mom who spends her weekends exploring a new hobby with her child, such as painting or learning to cook, fosters not only skills,

Family Reset:Building Eternal Bonds

but also a safe space to chat and strengthen emotional bonding.

Time with Spouse: Daily Food for Love

Love between couples is not immune to disconnection either. Many relationships are weakened because spouses believe that love stands on its own, without the need for ongoing attention. However, like any garden, love needs to be cultivated with small daily gestures, not only with special dates.

Practical example: A couple can establish a daily ritual, such as having a cup of tea together before bed, where they share thoughts about the day and give thanks for the moments lived. This simple act strengthens communication and reaffirms mutual commitment.

Transformation through presence

The story of Samuel and his father reminds us that it is never too late to redirect our time to what really matters. By building sacred moments and dedicating meaningful time, we are sowing love and connection that will transform not only our relationships, but also the legacy we leave.

Family Reset:Building Eternal Bonds

Pause today and ask yourself: **What changes can I make to be more present with those I love?** Remember that the time you give with intention is never in vain; it is an eternal investment in the hearts of those around you.

Tools to Transform the Home: Turning Time into Intentional Love

Time, more than a resource, is an expression of love. These practical tools are designed to help you build eternal bonds with your loved ones, making every moment shared meaningful and transformative.

🕯 Dating with Purpose: Revive Couple's Connection

Make your relationship a priority space by dedicating an exclusive moment to your partner each week. These quotations do not need to be elaborated; The important thing is that they are intentional, like when they were dating. A leisurely walk, a simple dinner at home, or a conversation without technological interruptions can rekindle emotional closeness.

Practical example: Imagine that, every Friday night, you turn off the TV and prepare a special dinner to share with your partner. You could talk about your dreams, reminisce about special moments, or just

Family Reset:Building Eternal Bonds

enjoy the silence together. This dedicated time fosters renewed love and fuels daily connection.

📖 The Family Soul Diary: Valuing the Meaningful

This journal is a weekly practice where each member writes down one thing they valued during the week. On Saturday night, everyone shares what they wrote, creating a space for gratitude and family reflection.

Practical example: Provide a special notebook for each family member to write down their reflections. For example, a child might write, "I appreciate that Mom helped me with my math homework," and a parent might share, "I appreciate my wife's patience this week." This exercise not only strengthens bonds, but also creates an environment of affirmation and love.

📖 Sacred Routines: Small Rituals, Deep Impact

Small rituals are the heart of the home. Praying together when you wake up, reading a psalm before going to sleep or sharing a special family breakfast, Sundays are simple gestures that strengthen relationships and spiritual bonds.

Family Reset:Building Eternal Bonds

Practical example: Before starting your day, gather your family for a short prayer. It could be something as simple as, "Lord, bless our day and our decisions." Or, on Sundays, prepare a special breakfast where everyone participates in the kitchen, creating not just a meal, but a shared memory.

🔘 The Sacred Hour Without Screens: Real Connection, Not Digital

Once a day, turn off all electronic devices. This time is dedicated exclusively to connecting as a family without technological interruptions.

Practical example: Every night after dinner, place the phones in a box or in a secluded place and use that time to play, talk or just be present with each other. This intentional act of digital disconnection promotes emotional connection.

🌰 Mini getaways: Memories that do not need a large investment

You don't need big budgets to create unforgettable memories. Sometimes an afternoon in the park, ice cream together, or stargazing can be more meaningful than a week in a hotel. The important thing is mindfulness during those moments.

Practical example: Surprise your family on a Saturday afternoon with a visit to the nearest park.

Family Reset:Building Eternal Bonds

Bring a ball, some snacks, and make time to enjoy the outdoors together. These spontaneous gestures create lasting memories and reinforce the sense of unity.

Jesus and Time as an Expression of Love: Following His Example

Jesus did not preach in a hurry. He walked with his family, ate with them, asked them questions and allowed them to feel part of his life. Their example teaches us that time spent with others is a transformative form of love. As Luke 16:10 says, "He who is faithful in a very little is faithful also in much; and he who is unjust in a very little is also unjust in a little thing." Being faithful in the small moments, like five minutes of mindfulness, can make all the difference for a lifetime.

Redeeming time, building the sky

Even though your home today may seem hectic, fragmented, or indifferent, you can still change your family's destiny. It all starts with something as simple and powerful as giving them your time. Remember, time does not stand still, but it can be redeemed. Every minute of tenderness, every shared lunch, every sustained silence and every

Family Reset:Building Eternal Bonds

prayer whispered in the family build a heaven on earth.

"Making good use of the time, because the days are bad." (Ephesians 5:16). Redeem your time. Make it a heaven. But eternal bonds are not built with theory, but with **living presence**.

Family Reset:Building Eternal Bonds

Chapter 4: The Transforming Power of Love
The Link That Holds the Sky

There is something that every human being longs for without saying it: **to love and be loved unconditionally**. Not for what he does, nor for what he offers, but for simply being. In homes where that love flows freely, there is an atmosphere that heals, restores, and reflects God's very presence.

But when love cools, words hurt, stares are avoided, and routine replaces tenderness. The home ceases to be a refuge and becomes a dry emotional field. For this reason, this chapter is an urgent invitation to **return to the beginning**, to the love that transforms, forgives, hopes and builds.

The Divine Origin of Family Love

God did not create man to be alone. He formed him in love, and to love. The first human act after creation was a relationship: male and female, flesh of their flesh, one in purpose.

"And the LORD God said, It is not good for a man to be alone; I will make him **a helper fit** for him." (Genesis 2:18)

Family Reset:Building Eternal Bonds

What can we say about this word "help-meet" and its meaning in the original language?

✍ In Genesis 2:18, the phrase "help-seeker" comes from the Hebrew *ezer kenegdo*. Let's discuss its original meaning and use in the Bible:

Original Meaning

- **Ezer**: This Hebrew word means "help" or "help." It does not imply subordination, but rather a powerful and essential help. In several biblical passages, *ezer* is used to describe God as the helper of his people, highlighting his strength and ability to provide support in times of need.
- **Kenegdo**: This term means "in front of him" or "corresponding to him". It indicates equality and complementarity, suggesting that women were created as a companion who corresponds perfectly to men.

The combination of *ezer kenegdo* in Genesis 2:18 reflects God's intention to provide man with a companion who is his equal, capable of supporting and complementing him in all aspects of life.

Use in the Bible

1. **Referring to women**: In Genesis 2:18, the phrase "help-meeting" is used specifically to describe the role of women in relation to men. This is the

Family Reset: Building Eternal Bonds

only place where this exact combination is used to refer to women.

2. **Referring to God**: The word *ezer* appears several times in the Bible to describe God as the helper of His people. For example:
   - Exodus 18:4: "My father's God was my helper *(ezer)* and delivered me from Pharaoh's sword."
   - Psalm 33:20: "Our soul waits for the Lord; He is our help *(Ezer)* and our shield."

In total, *ezer* is used more than 20 times in the Old Testament, and most of these references are to describe God.

Reflection

The use of *ezer kenegdo* to describe the woman in Genesis 2:18 should not be interpreted as an inferior position, but as a complementary and essential function. Just as God is a powerful helper to his people, woman is presented as an indispensable companion for man, designed to live in equality and harmony. ✍

From Eden, God established love as the foundation of the home. Ellen G. White said that Love is the beginning of heaven, and it should be the foundation of the home.

A home without love can have rules, routines, and religion... but it has no life. And where there is true love, God is present.

Family Reset:Building Eternal Bonds

When love wears out

Not all marriages are destroyed by infidelity. Many wither from emotional indifference. When the "I love you" is taken for granted. When hugs are replaced by commands. When children grow up without words of affirmation and without gestures of tenderness.

"But I have against you, who have left your first love." (Revelation 2:4)

This warning Jesus gave to a church can also resonate in our homes. It is not a matter of not loving, but of having forgotten how to love well.

Testimony: The reunion that began with flowers

Mario had been married for 18 years. One day, when he saw an old photo with his wife, he asked himself: "Where is all that we felt?" He began to bring her flowers every Friday, as when they were dating. At first, she was skeptical. But he didn't stop.

Over time, she began to wait for him with coffee, to look at him differently, to laugh again. Love had returned, not as an emotion, but as a renewed decision.

Family Reset:Building Eternal Bonds

How is the love that transforms expressed? The Essence of 1 Corinthians 13

True love, according to 1 Corinthians 13, is much more than a feeling; it is a decision that is reflected in actions and attitudes that transform the lives of those who receive it. This transcendent love has profound characteristics that guide us toward a way of living in connection with God and others:

- **Be patient:** Learn to wait calmly, even in times of conflict or difficulty.
- **It is benign:** It acts with kindness and always seeks the well-being of the other.
- **He does not seek his own:** He is selfless, prioritizing the needs of others over his own.
- **It endures everything:** It withstands trials and difficulties without giving up.
- **Never ceases:** Remains constant, even in the face of change or challenges.

"Love never faileth..." *(1 Corinthians* 13:8). This love never fails because it is not based on temporal circumstances, but on an eternal commitment.

Where there is genuine love, there will also be respect, tenderness, compassion, and forgiveness. These characteristics make love a healing power in the home and in human relationships.

Family Reset:Building Eternal Bonds

Characteristics of Transformative Love in Action

1. Patient love: Patience is not just waiting, but doing it calmly, without despair or judgment. This love accepts each other's imperfections and provides room for growth.

Practical example: When a child is learning a new skill and makes mistakes, a patient parent does not criticize or become impatient. Instead, he says, *"I know you can do it, keep trying."* This support strengthens your trust and relationship.

2. Kind love: Kindness translates into gestures that seek the well-being of others. This love thinks about how to make the lives of others lighter and more joyful.

Case in point: A mother who, after a long day at work, prepares her family's favorite food. Although tired, she does it with love because she knows that those small acts strengthen the bond.

3. Selfless love: True love does not seek its own benefit. It is a love that serves without expecting anything in return, always ready to sacrifice itself for others.

Case in point: A husband who dedicates his day off to organize a special activity for his partner, simply because he wants to see her smile. This act reinforces commitment and connection.

Family Reset: Building Eternal Bonds

4. Resilient love: She endures everything, from everyday conflicts to the darkest moments. This love does not give up or give up, but remains steadfast in the face of trials.

Practical example: A family that, facing economic difficulties, decides to pray together every day and support each other to move forward. This love in action creates hope and unity.

5. Constant love: It never stops being, even in the face of unexpected changes or difficult seasons. This love endures because it is rooted in eternal values.

Practical example: A couple facing a serious illness decides to strengthen their relationship, taking care of each other with love and dedication. Their commitment to each other becomes a reflection of God's eternal love.

Love as a transformative force

The love that transforms is the one that reflects patience, kindness, selflessness, endurance and perseverance. It does not depend on circumstance or merit, but on a genuine commitment to live by the divine principles of 1 Corinthians 13. This love, as Ellen G. White rightly expresses, brings with it respect, tenderness, compassion, and forgiveness, becoming the foundation of restored homes and strong relationships.

Family Reset:Building Eternal Bonds

Remember, love never fails. Every act of patience, kindness, and compassion is a step toward personal and family transformation. "Love never fails to be." (1 *Corinthians* 13:8) is not just a promise; it is a reality that can be lived out every day.

Tools to rekindle love at home:

Building bonds through intentional gestures

Love in the home does not stand alone; It needs to be cultivated and nurtured with small daily acts that reflect attention, tenderness, and purpose. These tools are designed to strengthen family relationships, allowing each member to feel valued and loved in a unique way.

♥ Love Languages: Discovering How Each Member Feels Loved

Each person experiences love differently. Understanding the love languages in your family is key to connecting on a deep level. Identify how each member feels most loved: through words of affirmation, quality time, gifts, acts of service, or physical touch.

Practical example: Observe how your children or your partner react. If your child smiles every time you give them a compliment, their language can be

Family Reset: Building Eternal Bonds

words of affirmation. If your partner loves it when you cook something special, maybe acts of service are their language. Use this information to personalize your gestures of affection.

Reflection: When you give love in the language that the other person understands best, you are building a bridge that connects their needs with your intention to love.

💬 Quotes that heal: The power of positive words

Words have a direct impact on emotions and household dynamics. Repeating phrases such as, *"I care about you," "Thank you for being here,"* or *"I'm proud of you"* can heal wounds, strengthen self-esteem, and create an environment of affirmation.

Practical example: Before you leave for work, tell your child, *"I trust you, and I know you'll do your best today."* Or to your partner: *"I appreciate everything you do for us."* These simple, yet powerful phrases transform the emotional environment of the home.

Reflection: Words cost nothing, but their impact can be eternal. Use them with intention to sow life and love.

Family Reset: Building Eternal Bonds

Sacred Embrace: Healing Through Physical Gestures

A 30-second hug a day has both emotional and spiritual healing effects. This simple gesture creates a connection that transcends words and conveys security, love, and acceptance.

Practical example: At the beginning or end of the day, hug your children or your partner for a few seconds. As you do so, say in your mind, "*I love you, and I'm here for you.*" This simple act can relieve tension and convey peace.

Reflection: Physical gestures are silent languages that speak directly to the heart. Never underestimate the power of a hug.

Family Dates: Exclusive Moments of Connection

Once a week, schedule an exclusive time to be with your partner or with your children. You don't need to leave the house or do something expensive; the important thing is the intention to dedicate time to them without distractions.

Practical example: Organize a picnic in the yard, a board game, or watch a movie together while enjoying popcorn. Let them know that that time is

Family Reset:Building Eternal Bonds

just for them and that you wouldn't trade those moments for anything.

Reflection: Family dating nurtures relationships in intentional ways. They are spaces where bonds are strengthened and hearts are connected.

💜 Handwritten Love Letters: Expressions of Affection That Last

Writing a short letter expressing admiration, affection and gratitude is an invaluable gift that is never discarded. This intentional gesture shows your loved ones what you appreciate in them and strengthens their sense of worth.

Practical example: Write a letter to your child saying, "I love how you always help with a smile. I'm so proud of you." Or to your partner: "Thank you for being my refuge and for all you do for our family. Your love inspires me every day." These words become a treasure that you can read and reread when you need encouragement.

Reflection: A handwritten letter has the power to capture feelings eternally. It is a legacy of love that they can always keep.

Rekindling Love with Intention

Family Reset:Building Eternal Bonds

These tools are more than acts; They are intentional expressions of love that can transform the home environment and strengthen family bonds. Remember that love is not demanded, it is cultivated. Through words, gestures, time, and gratitude, you are sowing seeds that will blossom into strong, eternal relationships.

Love Doesn't Erase Conflict, But It Heals the Environment: Transforming Relationships with Safe Love

True love does not eliminate differences or challenges. However, it creates a safe environment in which differences can be faced with respect, compassion, and acceptance. In a home where you love deeply:

You can fail without fear of rejection: Imperfections are accepted as part of growth.

You can tell the truth without being judged: Sincerity is received with openness, without criticism or condemnation.

You can start over without pride: Forgiveness flows and connection is prioritized over ego.

As Proverbs 15:1 teaches: "A gentle answer takes away anger; But the harsh word makes the fury rise." This principle invites us to respond with gentleness and love, defusing tensions and creating a peaceful environment in the home.

Family Reset:Building Eternal Bonds

Love as a transformative force

Love doesn't just heal relationships; It is the strongest power in the universe. It is the force that brought Jesus to this earth, the essence that sustains heaven and the ingredient that can make your home a piece of paradise. Love transforms because it creates a space where differences do not divide, but rather nurture and strengthen bonds.

Case in point: Imagine a home where a child feels safe admitting a mistake, such as getting bad grades. Instead of yelling, parents respond with love by saying, "*We know you can do better. We're here to help you achieve that.*" This approach not only corrects the problem, but also strengthens the relationship.

Don't expect it to be born alone: Choose to sow it every day

Love does not arise spontaneously; It requires intention and action. It is cultivated in words that edify, in gestures that nourish and in decisions that prioritize relationships over circumstances. Sowing love is a daily commitment that, over time, transforms the atmosphere of the home.

Practical example: Take five minutes a day to express gratitude or affirmation to your loved ones. For example, tell your partner, "*Thank you for always*

Family Reset:Building Eternal Bonds

being there for us," or your child, *"I'm so proud of your effort in school."* These little seeds of love bloom strongly when they are sown consistently.

When love returns, so does heaven

Love doesn't just resolve conflicts; it transforms them into opportunities to grow together. It is a daily decision that is reflected in every word, gesture and choice. When we allow love to guide our actions, our home becomes a reflection of heaven, a place where peace, safety, and compassion are part of the routine.

Remember, love never fails. Every small act of tenderness and understanding is a step toward a heaven-breathing home on earth.

Family Reset: Building Eternal Bonds

Chapter 5: The Transformative Power of Communication

Restoring Bridges in the Family Soul

In the beginning was the word. Thus begins the most sacred story. Not with an act of force, but with a voice:

"And God said, Let there be light; and there was light." (Genesis 1:3) **God spoke... and the universe was born.**

And if the universe was created by a word, it is not surprising that families are also built – or destroyed – by words. Communication is the invisible breath that binds hearts together. When it is interrupted, the home begins to die silently.

This chapter is not a theory about how to speak. It is an invitation to return, to look into each other's eyes, to restore bridges broken by years of silence, shouting or indifference. But speaking well is not just saying the right things... that is to say them with love, in time, and with the intention of healing.

When words unite... or hurt

Rebeca and Jorge had been married for twenty years. They lived in the same house, but they were two islands. She would say, "He never listens to me." And he said, "She's always upset, whatever she says." In therapy, conversation was a minefield.

Family Reset:Building Eternal Bonds

There were so many "nevers", "alwayss", "you make me", "you ignore me" that it was impossible to move forward.

Until I asked them a question: "When was the last time you said "thank you"? They looked at each other... and they did not remember.

The gratitude had evaporated. The jokes too. The words of affirmation were a distant memory. And what hurt the most... they didn't know how to get back.

The Divine Model of Communication

The Bible is full of dialogue. God spoke to Adam, to Moses, to Samuel, to Mary. Jesus never left the crowds speechless. But more than preaching, He **listened**. To the Samaritan woman, to the centurion, to the blind man, to his confused disciples. He asked, waited, answered with grace.

"Golden apple with silver figures is the word spoken as it should be." (Proverbs 25:11)

Jesus modeled communication that heals: empathetic, clear, patient, and with eternal purpose.

Family Reset:Building Eternal Bonds

Signs that communication is broken

- There is a lot of talk, but nothing is said.
- It is discussed without listening.
- Blame is thrown, no responsibility is taken.
- Silence is kept out of resentment, not peace.
- What the other did not say is interpreted, but what he or she did say is ignored.

These are cracks in the soul of the home. But every crack is also a door. The question is not whether you have communication problems, but whether you are willing to **heal them through love**.

Example: A child who just needed to be heard

Carlos was 14 years old. His mother said he was rebellious, disobedient, and cold. When we spoke alone, he only said, "I wish you would listen to me without sermons."

I asked him to write a letter to his parents. She cried as she read it. The letter had no complaints... I was in pain. Said:

"Sometimes I talk, but I've already learned his answers. So I'd better shut up."

That letter transformed his mother. He began to listen to it five minutes a day without interrupting. Two months later, Carlos smiled again. **He had been heard... finally.**

Family Reset: Building Eternal Bonds
Tools to restore communication in your home

💬 **Active listening**: Repeat what the other person said in your own words and ask, "Is that what you meant?"

💭 **The three-second rule**: Before responding in a tense conversation, breathe, pray, and count to three. Patience avoids wounds.

🕊 **The altar of dialogue**: One night a week, sit down as a couple or family to share what you have experienced. No screens. Only with an open heart.

💟 **Letters from the soul**: Sometimes what cannot be said out loud, can be written. Start a family notebook of anonymous letters.

📦 **The Forgiveness Box**: When there is an argument, write down the offense, put it in a box. In the evening, read them and ask for forgiveness, then burn the paper as a symbol of restoration.

Quotes from Wisdom

"Harsh words are like arrows." Tender words are like a balm. With them you can heal, or you can destroy." (*The Ministry of Kindness*, p. 19)

"Death and life are in the power of the tongue, and he who loves it will eat of its fruits." (Proverbs 18:21)

Family Reset:Building Eternal Bonds

A family that does not communicate, does not grow. But a family that learns to speak with respect, tenderness and humility has all heaven in its favor.

Today you can start with a simple phrase: "Sorry for what I said." I love you more than I expressed."

And that phrase can change everything.

Family Reset:Building Eternal Bonds

Family Reset: Building Eternal Bonds

Chapter 6: The Transforming Power of Prayer

The Invisible Altar That Supports the Home: A Call to Prayer as a Spiritual Center

If we could walk into a home and see nothing but its spiritual atmosphere, what would we find? An altar lit, vibrating with prayers that rise daily, or a fire extinguished years ago? A constant whisper that connects the heart of the family with heaven, or a silence that weighs on the walls, gradually extinguishing the spiritual life of the home?

Prayer is not just a tradition forgotten by modernity; it is the artery that connects the heart of the home to heaven. Where there is prayer, there is divine presence. Where it is lacking, the house may be physically full, but spiritually empty. This call is not to pray more as an obligation, but to rekindle **the invisible altar** that provides direction, life, and eternal protection to the home.

The Altar of the Home: Restoring God's Original Plan

From the beginning, God's desire was always to dwell among His people, not as a distant or unapproachable figure, but as a **friend of the soul**.

Family Reset:Building Eternal Bonds

When he designed the home, he thought of it as a living temple:

- Every parent is a priest who guides spiritually.
- Every mother, a worshipper who inspires with faith and love.
- Each child, a living offering dedicated to Him.

God declared, "And they will make a sanctuary for me, and I will dwell in their midst." (Exodus 25:8). His longing is not limited to living in churches on weekends, but to be present in rooms where people talk with love, in dining rooms where they pray in unity and in rooms where His name is invoked with faith and hope.

Practical example: Transform a corner of your home into a visible space for prayer. It doesn't have to be big or elaborate; a place with an open Bible, candle, or inspiring picture can remind the family that this is a sanctuary where God dwells.

Ellen G. White, in her book *Counsels for the Church*, reminds us that family prayer is more sacred than any other duty. It is the key to unlocking God's blessing upon the home.

Family Reset: Building Eternal Bonds

This message reinforces that the strength of the home lies not in its physical structure, but in the daily commitment to connect with God.

Lighting the Invisible Altar Again: Practical Steps

1. **Set a family prayer schedule:** .Start with something simple, such as praying together before meals or at the end of the day. This daily act establishes a sacred routine that invites the divine presence into the home.

Practical example: Before bedtime, gather the family in a circle and allow each member to share a short prayer. Even the little ones can participate by saying something they're grateful for.

2. **Creates a spiritual environment in the home:** Prayer is nurtured by an environment that reflects peace and purpose. Keep the home a space where conversations, gestures, and decisions reflect a spirit of gratitude and love.

Practical example: Take time to reflect as a family on a weekly verse, such as Psalm 127:1 (NIV): "*Unless the Lord builds the house, those who build it labor in vain.*" Each member can share how to apply it in their lives.

3. **Make prayer a living, non-mechanical experience:**

Family Reset:Building Eternal Bonds

Prayer should not feel like a chore, but like a real conversation with God. Speak from the heart, give thanks for the blessings of the day, and present the needs of the family with sincerity.

Practical example: Invite each member to write a short sentence on a piece of paper and place it in a visible place, such as the refrigerator, so that everyone can remember it during the week.

Making the Home a Reflection of Heaven: Lighting the Invisible Altar

The invisible altar that supports the hearth cannot be seen with physical eyes, but its impact is felt deeply in the spiritual atmosphere. It is perceived in the peace that fills every corner, in the love that guides relationships and in the faith that is shared among its members. Restoring the practice of family prayer not only connects the heart of the home to heaven, but also strengthens the bonds that bind the family together, creating a space where God's presence becomes tangible.

The Altar: More Than a Practice, a Divine Purpose

A home without prayer may seem busy and inhabited, but it is spiritually empty. The family altar is not just a routine activity; It is the heart that

Family Reset:Building Eternal Bonds

gives life to the home, filling it with direction, protection, and eternal purpose. This invisible altar transforms family dynamics because it places God at the center, not as an occasional visitor, but as the foundation of every decision and every relationship.

Practical example: Take a moment each day to pray together as a family, perhaps after dinner or before bed. Even if not everyone participates at first, your consistency can inspire others to join in. Make that time a sacred space to express gratitude, present needs, and renew spiritual connection.

Transforming the ordinary into the eternal

When God dwells in the home, what seems simple and everyday becomes eternal. From a conversation in the dining room to decisions made as a family, everything can reflect divine light when His name is called upon in faith. This process is not automatic; it requires intention, perseverance and commitment from those who make up the household.

Practical example: Identify a space in your home where you can place an open Bible, candle, or spiritual symbol. This small corner acts as a physical reminder of the invisible altar and helps to maintain focus on God's presence in daily life.

Family Reset:Building Eternal Bonds
Choose to light this invisible altar

Restoring the spiritual atmosphere of your home is not just an individual act; It is an invitation to the whole family to build together a sanctuary of love and faith. Choose to light this invisible altar each day with simple yet purposeful acts: from a shared prayer to a word of affirmation. With each step, you will be allowing God's presence to transform the ordinary into something eternal.

When Prayer Disappears from the Home: A Call to Restore the Spiritual Walls

A lack of prayer in the home does not always begin with a conscious decision. Often, it starts in subtle ways: because of tiredness, the monotony of daily routines, or even the false belief that it's no longer necessary. However, when prayer is extinguished, something deeper is affected. Parents stop praying, and children, on many occasions, stop believing. Faith, instead of being a living force, becomes an empty tradition, something that exists only in name, but lacks essence.

"A home without prayer is like a city without walls." This metaphor shows us how vulnerable a home that does not seek divine protection becomes. Without prayer, the walls that protect the family

Family Reset:Building Eternal Bonds

spiritually weaken, leaving room for division, discouragement, and the influence of the enemy.

The Effect of Absence of Prayer in the Home

1. **Spiritual disconnection:** Prayer is the bridge that connects home to heaven. Without it, home may seem busy and active, but spiritually empty. Decisions are made without divine direction, and God's presence feels far away.

Thoughtful example: Think of a home where dinners used to include a prayer of thanks. Over time, that habit was put aside by haste or distractions. Gradually, the family stops reflecting on their blessings and begins to focus on everyday challenges, losing the peace that connection with God brings.

2. **Impact on children:** When children grow up in a home without prayer, it is easier for them to see faith as something without practical relevance. The absence of living examples of spirituality in the home can cause them to see religion as an empty tradition, rather than an active relationship with God.

Family Reset:Building Eternal Bonds

Practical example: A mother or father can take a few minutes before the children fall asleep to pray for them and with them. Hearing a parent say, "*Lord, take care of my children, guide them, and give them wisdom,*" leaves a deep imprint on your heart and nurtures your faith.

3. **Emotional and spiritual vulnerability:** Without prayer, life's challenges seem greater and the strength of home is depleted faster. Prayer does not eliminate problems, but it strengthens the family to face them with hope and unity.

Thoughtful example: A family experiencing financial hardship may be fragmented by stress. But if they choose to gather together in daily prayer, presenting their concerns to God, they will find spiritual strength and comfort in his presence, strengthening their unity in the face of adversity.

Restoring the Home Altar: How to Recover Prayer?

1. **Make prayer a priority:** Decide to start with small steps. A short prayer in the morning or before bed can make all the difference. No matter how busy the routine is, there is always room to connect with God.

Family Reset:Building Eternal Bonds

2. **Involve the whole family:** Invite the children and your partner to participate in the prayers. Let everyone present their own requests, so that everyone feels that they are an active part of the family altar.

Practical example: One night a week, create a "prayer circle," where each member shares something for which he or she is grateful and something for which he or she needs divine help.

3. **Pray sincerely, not out of obligation:** Prayer should not feel like a duty, but as a moment of connection. Talk to God in your own words, thanking you, asking for guidance, and presenting your concerns.

A home protected by spiritual walls

When prayer disappears, the home loses more than just a routine; he loses his deepest connection with God. However, it is never too late to relight this invisible altar. Prayer is the shield that protects the family, the bond that unites them and the force that guides them.

Restoring the practice of prayer does not require immediate big changes, just small constant acts of faith. With every whisper to heaven, every thank you spoken and every petition submitted, the walls of the home become stronger and the atmosphere of the home is transformed into a reflection of the sky.

Family Reset:Building Eternal Bonds

Testimonial: A Mother on Her Knees – The Transformative Power of Prayer

I met Elena, a simple woman with an extraordinary story. She raised four children alone under challenging circumstances. Without a steady salary or a college degree, their material resources were limited. But it had something far more powerful than any earthly wealth: an altar lit by prayer.

Every morning, without fail, Ellen prayed by name and out of necessity, interceding for each of her children with unwavering faith. I once confessed with humility and conviction, *"I don't have much to leave you, but I have accumulated prayer for each one."*

Elena's Legacy: Children Shaped by Faith

Today, Elena's children are men and women of faith. Some are pastors, some are missionaries, and some are professionals whose lives are dedicated to serving with purpose and compassion. Its success is not the result of chance, but of a home sustained by the spiritual strength that only prayer can provide.

Thoughtful example: Every night before bed, Elena would take time to mention her children's concerns in her prayers: school struggles, difficult decisions, and dreams they had. For her, prayer was not just a religious act, but a tangible way to guide and protect her family. That example shaped the character and

Family Reset: Building Eternal Bonds

faith of their children, leaving them an eternal legacy.

The Burning Altar: The Key to Eternal Impact

Elena's secret lay not in her external circumstances, but in her perseverance to keep the invisible altar of prayer burning. This altar was the pillar of his home and the foundation upon which he built a legacy of unwavering faith.

Practical lesson: If today you feel that your resources or skills are insufficient, remember that a lit altar is enough to transform lives. Spend a few minutes each day praying for your family, presenting their names and needs to God. This act, although simple, has the power to move mountains and change destinies.

The Power of Intercession in Action

Elena's testimony teaches us that the greatest love we can offer our family is not in riches or titles, but in sincere and constant prayers. Every cry to heaven is like a seed sown in the hearts of those we love, a seed that will grow and bear fruit in its time.

The Spiritual Power of Praying Together: Transformation and Unity in the Home

Family Reset:Building Eternal Bonds

Jesus left us a powerful promise in Matthew 18:20: *"For where two or three are gathered together in my name, there am I in the midst of them."* When a family prays together, it is not only strengthening its emotional bonds; it is opening the doors for the divine presence to dwell in their home. Prayer in unity transcends the logical and allows divine promises to be activated, transforming the spiritual environment of the family.

Impacts of Praying in Unity

1. Spiritual bond is strengthened: Prayer together is more than words; it is an experience that unites hearts under a shared purpose. When a family prays together, they feel part of something bigger than themselves.

Practical example: Before starting each week, gather your family for a group prayer where each member presents a specific request or gives thanks for something they have experienced. This act of spiritual unity will strengthen the sense of belonging and shared faith.

2. Promises of protection are activated: Family prayer is a spiritual shield that protects the home from negative influences and provides security. By calling on God's name together, divine blessings and care are activated upon each member.

Family Reset:Building Eternal Bonds

Practical example: Take a moment each night to pray for the protection of each family member. For example, say, "*Lord, guard us while we sleep and guide our decisions tomorrow.*" This habit not only brings comfort, but also creates an environment of peace.

3. Children's hearts are opened: Children and adolescents who participate in family prayers tend to open their hearts more easily. The practice of praying together helps you express your emotions, dreams, and worries in a safe space.

Practical example: During prayer, allow children to share a concern or something they are grateful for. This emotional openness builds confidence and strengthens their faith.

4. Conflict is reduced and empathy is increased: Prayer not only connects with God; it also eases tensions in the home. When a family prays together, differences are faced with greater empathy and conflicts are transformed into opportunities to grow together.

Practical example: If there is a conflict in the home, before you try to resolve it, gather your family for a short prayer. Ask for wisdom and understanding. This act defuses tensions and helps to approach problems from a more loving perspective.

5. God becomes the center of decisions: When a family prays together, it places God as the architect

Family Reset: Building Eternal Bonds

of its home and its plans. This not only builds trust, but also guides decisions toward God's purpose.

Practical example: Before making important decisions such as moving, changing jobs, or school decisions, gather with your family to pray for direction and clarity. This habit places God at the center of family life.

Prayer as a pillar of the home

Joint prayer has the power to transform the home into a reflection of heaven. By strengthening the spiritual bond, activating divine promises, opening hearts, reducing conflict, and centering decisions on God, a space of love, peace, and eternal purpose is created. The unity that is built in each shared prayer leaves a legacy that transcends generations.

Remember, the strength of a family lies not only in their physical union, but in their spiritual connection.

Practical Tools for Restoring the Family Altar: Renewing the Spiritual Connection in the Home

Restoring the family altar is an invitation to strengthen the relationship with God and among family members. These practical tools are simple, yet powerful, ways to rekindle the spiritual

Family Reset: Building Eternal Bonds

atmosphere in the home, creating a space where faith and love are at the center.

🜄 10 Minutes That Change the Day: Spiritual Routine to Start and End Together

Set aside a set time each day to connect with God as a family, even if it's just 10 minutes. Divide that time into 5 minutes when you wake up and 5 minutes when you go to bed. Read a verse, pray aloud, be thankful for blessings, present your requests, and turn the day over to God.

Practical example: In the morning, before each member leaves home, gather to read a verse such as Psalm 118:24: *"This is the day which the Lord made; we will rejoice and rejoice in him."* Close with a short prayer, asking for wisdom and blessing. At night, meet again to give thanks for what you have experienced.

Reflection: These small daily moments not only connect with God, but also create a sense of purpose and unity in the family.

📖 Family Reading of Promises: Living Under the Word

Choose a weekly Bible promise that inspires and guides your family. Write it down in a visible place,

Family Reset: Building Eternal Bonds

such as the fridge, so that everyone remembers it and repeats it together every day. Let that Word influence the decisions and attitudes of the week.

Practical example: A promise like Isaiah 41:10, *"Do not be afraid, for I am with you,"* can serve as a constant reminder of God's presence. At the end of the week, reflect on how that promise was fulfilled in your lives and share experiences.

Reflection: Living under a promise creates an atmosphere of trust in God and spiritual strength in the home.

The Family Prayer Notebook: Recording God's Faithfulness

A family prayer notebook is a powerful tool for recording requests and, over time, recording how God responds to them. Seeing prayers answered strengthens faith and evidences God's active presence in their lives.

Practical example: Dedicate a page to each family member, noting their specific requests and the date they submit them. As prayers are answered, add notes of gratitude. For example: *"On March 5 we prayed for a new job, and God opened a door on March 15."*

Family Reset:Building Eternal Bonds

Reflection: This record not only documents God's faithfulness, but also motivates us to continue trusting and praying together.

🕊 The Sacred Corner: A Visible Space to Seek God

Designate a special place in your home where you can pray. No matter the size; it can be a corner with an open Bible, a candle, or a symbol that inspires us to seek God. This sacred corner will be recognized as the place of encounter with the divine.

Practical example: Choose a quiet space and decorate it with simplicity: a small table with a Bible, a prayer notebook, a candle and perhaps a plant. Whenever someone needs a moment of reflection or comfort, they will know that that corner is available for prayer.

Reflection: Having a dedicated space helps create a routine and encourages spirituality as part of daily life.

🌑 Monthly Cry Day: A Special Appointment with God in the Family

Once a month, host a special home worship service to pray as a family, hear praise, share testimonies,

Family Reset: Building Eternal Bonds

and focus prayers on a common purpose. This day can be a source of renewal and spiritual joy.

Practical example: One Sunday a month, gather the family to listen to inspiring songs, share how God has worked in their lives during the month, and pray for specific goals such as spiritual growth, healing, or reconciliation. End the day by dining together with gratitude.

Reflection: This day strengthens family bonds and renews the focus on God as the center of their lives.

Renovating the Family Altar Day by Day: Small Steps to Transform the Home.

Restoring the family altar does not require grand gestures, but the intention of building a space where God's presence is the center on a daily basis. With simple tools like prayer, gratitude, and fellowship, your home can become a reflection of heaven, a place of peace, unity, and divine purpose.

Practical example: Take time in the morning and evening to gather your family and read a verse together, pray, and express gratitude for the blessings of the day. This act, though simple, establishes a spiritual routine that transforms the atmosphere of the home.

Family Reset:Building Eternal Bonds

Praying When No One Wants to Pray Anymore: The Strength of Perseverance

What happens when you are the only person in your household who keeps practicing prayer? When have your children lost faith or does your partner respond with indifference or even mockery? Although it may seem difficult, the answer is clear: pray stronger, firmer, and more faithfully. Individual intercession has an extraordinary power that transcends human logic.

God promises, *"And all your children shall be taught of the Lord; and he will multiply the peace of your children"* (Isaiah 54:13). This promise is a light of hope that sustains those who cry out for the restoration of their families.

Practical example: Dedicate a specific space in your home as your prayer corner. Even if others don't participate, keep the invisible altar burning through heartfelt supplications, mentioning each member of your family by name and need. This practice, constant and steadfast, is the channel through which God can reach their hearts.

Ellen G. White, in her book *The Ministry of Healing*, spoke directly to mothers, saying that a mother who prays—even alone—can become the channel through which God reaches an entire family

Family Reset:Building Eternal Bonds

Even when it seems like there's no support, your faithfulness in prayer can sow spiritual seeds that will flourish in their time.

Transformation through the family altar

Prayer is more than words; It is a flame that illuminates the home, dispels darkness, and restores purpose. When the family altar is active, character is formed, wounds are healed, and bonds are strengthened. No matter how difficult the environment may seem, every act of prayer, gratitude, and faith has the power to transform not only your home, but also the world around you.

The Impact of Solitary Prayer: A Channel of Transformation

Even if you are alone in your home, your prayer is a channel through which God can work in the hearts of your family. Intercession, even when it has no visible support, reaches spiritual dimensions that generate profound changes, visible at the time.

Practical example: Dedicate a quiet corner of your house as your personal altar. Pray each day, mentioning the names and needs of each member of your family. Even if they don't participate, your prayers will have a quiet but powerful effect on their lives.

Family Reset: Building Eternal Bonds

The Flame That Dispels Darkness: The Transforming Power of Prayer

Prayer is not simply a routine; It is a flame that warms a cold home, illuminates the darkest moments and chases away discouragement. Even if you feel alone in this act, every word spoken in faith can bring light and renewal to the atmosphere of your home. Darkness never resists an interceding family.

Practical example: Pray for the unity and salvation of your family before they fall asleep. Use biblical promises as a basis for your requests, such as Psalm 91: *"He who dwells in the shelter of the Most High shall dwell under the shadow of the Almighty."*

Bend Your Knees, Transform the World: The Eternal Impact of Prayer

You don't need great wealth or a perfect home to see a significant change in your family. Nor do you need ideal conditions or extraordinary material resources. All you really need is to **bend your knees in prayer** and keep the family altar lit. It is in this sacred space of connection with God that **character is formed, wounds are healed, bonds are strengthened**, and relationships begin to reflect heaven here on earth.

Family Reset: Building Eternal Bonds

Prayer not only transforms the practitioner; it also has the power to **soften hearts and renew the spiritual atmosphere of the home**. Like water fertilizing barren land, constant prayer can bring life to places where there seemed to be dryness and distance.

The Family Altar: A Source of Renewal and Peace

The family altar is a symbolic place that represents the ongoing search for God's presence in the home. Through prayer, we transform our everyday spaces into a sanctuary where love, peace, and faith can flourish.

Practical example: Take a few minutes each night to pray as a family, mentioning specific thanks and requests. Even if they start with little time, the simple act of joining their voices in clamor creates an atmosphere of unity and purpose.

Prayer as water for an arid terrain

If your home seems spiritually dry, don't be discouraged. Remember that **persistent prayer is like water for an arid terrain**, capable of regenerating what seemed lost. Every prayer spoken in faith is a seed that, in time, will bear fruit.

Family Reset: Building Eternal Bonds

Thoughtful example: A mother or father who constantly prays for their children, even without receiving an immediate response, is planting spiritual roots. With patience and faith, you will see how those prayers impact your family's lives in God's perfect timing.

Prayer as an engine of change

The world begins to transform from the altar of the home. You don't need to wait for ideal conditions or have abundant resources; it is enough to give God in prayer every day. Bending your knees and keeping this spiritual flame burning will not only heal your home, but it will be the starting point for impacting the world around you.

"Cry unto me, and I will answer thee, and teach thee great and hidden things which thou knowest not." (Jeremiah 33:3, RVR1960). This call reminds us of the power and promise of seeking God with constancy and faith.

The Family Altar: A Transformation Center

The family prayer altar is not a physical place, but an ongoing commitment to surrender the home to God. It is the space where your words, your supplications, and your faith become instruments of divine change.

Family Reset: Building Eternal Bonds

Practical example: Choose a specific time of day to pray with your family or, if you are alone, to intercede for each member of the household. Mention their names, their needs, and present your home as an offering to God. For example, you might say, "*Lord, bless our relationships, give us wisdom to love each other better, and make our home a reflection of Your love.*"

Prayer as water for an arid terrain

If you feel like your home is spiritually dry or disconnected, don't lose hope. Remember that prayer is like water that slowly penetrates the earth, fertilizing it and preparing it to bear fruit. Although the results may not be immediate, each prayer is a seed that will eventually blossom.

Reflective example: Imagine a mother praying alone in a room for her children, while they are not participating. Even if you don't see it or understand it in the moment, that prayer is planting deep roots that, in the perfect time, will bring visible results in your lives.

Transformation Begins at the Altar

The world begins to change from the altar of the home. It is there that the foundations of a united, strong family are built, led by eternal principles. Persistent prayer doesn't just transform homes; it

Family Reset:Building Eternal Bonds

also impacts communities, generations, and the entire world.

If you want to see a sky in your home, you don't need to buy more stuff or look for great external solutions. Bend your knees and seek God's presence with faith and constancy. From that invisible altar strength will be renewed, relationships will be restored and discouragement will give way to hope.

Family Reset:Building Eternal Bonds

Family Reset: Building Eternal Bonds

Chapter 7: The Restoration of the Lost Sons

From Grief to Family Redemption

Few prayers carry as much anguish as this: **"Lord... bring it back."**

It is not a matter of a son who left physically, but of the one who is there, but is no longer the same. The one who stopped believing. The one who stopped talking. The one who stopped trusting. The one who lives under the same roof, but with an invisible wall between his soul and yours.

This chapter is for you, mother who prays at dawn. Father who hides his tears. Grandfather who is still waiting. It's not too late. **God still writes stories of redemption.**

The prodigal son continues to walk our streets

Jesus did not tell the parable of the prodigal son as a distant story. He told it because he knew that many homes would experience that same scene: A son who moves away. A father who remains at the door waiting. A house that longs for hugs that do not come.

"And he got up and came to his father. And while he was still a long way off, his father saw him, and he

Family Reset: Building Eternal Bonds

was moved with mercy, and he ran, and threw himself on his neck, and kissed him." (Luke 15:20)

Restoration begins with compassion... **not with reproach**. The love that restores is the love that waits with open arms, even when the heart is bleeding.

When children get lost inside the home

Not all lost children are physically far away. Some live with you... but they are no longer there. They live on the screen. In his wounds. In its isolation. They left without packing their bags, but they carry their souls loaded.

Sometimes it was divorce. Others, the excess of control. Perhaps silent abuse, or simply the absence of words of affirmation. Whatever the cause, it **is not a matter of looking for culprits, but of looking for ways of restoration.**

"Mothers and fathers need to remember that they themselves have done many things that have contributed to making their children who they are." (*The Adventist Home*, p. 303)

Testimony: A Daughter, a Diary, a Redemption

Family Reset:Building Eternal Bonds

Isabela was moving further and further away from her mother. Long silences, curt answers, no sign of affection. Until one day, her mother found an old diary: "I would like my mother to listen to me without correcting me... to tell me that she is proud of me."

Those words changed their deal. He began to hug her without asking for an explanation. To invite it without imposing. To pray for her... with tears, not with anger.

A year later, Isabela returned to the ways of Señor.La mother told me, "The Holy Spirit showed me that I did not need to win her with sermons, but with tenderness."

Steps towards restoring bonds with your children

Rebuilding bonds with your children is a process that requires humility, patience, and intentional love. These steps will help you renew the emotional and spiritual connection that may have weakened over time.

1. Ask for forgiveness, even if you don't feel guilty

Acknowledging possible wounds or moments of disconnection, even if they are not intentional, can open doors that had been closed. Sometimes a

Family Reset:Building Eternal Bonds

simple "I'm sorry if I failed" has more power than any advice. This humble action disarms pride and creates an atmosphere of openness.

Practical example: If you feel distance from your child, say, "I want to apologize if at some point I didn't listen to you or I failed you. My wish is that we will build a stronger connection again." This act of humility can be the first step toward sincere reconciliation.

2. Pray for them by name, need, and purpose

Prayer has a profound impact, both on the children and on the heart of the one who prays. By presenting their names and specific needs before God, you are sowing intercession that can transform lives.

"The effectual prayer of the righteous avails much." (James 5:16, RVR1960).

Practical example: Create a prayer list with your children's names and their current needs. Pray for them daily, saying, "*Lord, guide [name], protect it, and direct it toward Your eternal purpose.*" These constant supplications are seeds that will bear fruit in their time.

Family Reset:Building Eternal Bonds

3. Invite them, don't force them

Jesus did not force anyone's heart; He came with love and patience, saying, "Behold, I stand at the door and knock; if anyone hears my voice and opens the door, I will go in to him and dine with him, and he with me." (Revelation 3:20, RVR1960). Inviting your children, rather than imposing on them, fosters a relationship of respect and trust.

Practical example: Instead of requiring them to participate in family or spiritual activities, invite them tenderly. For example, *"Would you like us to read this verse together? I'd love to hear what you think."* This approach creates an environment where they feel valued and respected.

4. Find emotional bridges

Emotional connection can open the spiritual channel. Look for activities, memories, or experiences that can serve as bridges to strengthen your relationship.

Practical example: If your child enjoys music, share a song that has a positive or meaningful message. If you have shared memories of a special place, suggest visiting it together. These moments of

Family Reset: Building Eternal Bonds

connection reinforce the emotional bonds that are the foundation of the relationship.

5. Love unconditionally, but with hope

True love never goes out, even when there are disagreements. Even if you don't approve of the wrong decisions, don't stop expressing love and hope toward them. This balance between firmness and tenderness is what helps to guide without judgment.

Practical example: If your child is facing spiritual or emotional struggles, say, "*No matter what, I'll always be here for you. My love for you will never change.*" These words remind them that your support is unconditional, but always full of hope.

Rebuilding with humility and purpose

Renewing bonds with your children isn't always easy, but these steps will help you build a path to healing and restoration. With constant prayer, respectful invitations, and unconditional love, you can reflect God's love in their lives. As Jesus taught us, connection to the heart is the first step in restoring any relationship.

Family Reset: Building Eternal Bonds

Practical tools for parent advocates:
Strengthening bonds through love and prayer

As parent advocates, we have the power to transform our children's lives through intentional acts of love, communication, and prayer. These practical tools are designed to help you deepen your emotional and spiritual connection with them, leaving an impact that transcends time.

🫐 The Intercessory Notebook: Prayers That Transcend

An intercession notebook is a dedicated place to record prayers, biblical promises, dreams, and answers related to your children. This habit creates a tangible record of the spiritual care you offer them and allows you to reflect on how God works in their lives.

Practical example: Write your child's name on a page and add specific sentences for their life. For example: *"Lord, guide [name] in his school decisions and protect him from all negative influences."* It also records the moments when these prayers are answered as a testimony of God's faithfulness.

Family Reset: Building Eternal Bonds

👂 The Five Minutes Without Judgment: Active and Loving Listening

Dedicate a space each day for your child to speak freely, without interruptions, without sermons and without immediate reactions. This time allows them to express their emotions and thoughts without fear of criticism, fostering trust and understanding.

Practical example: During those five minutes, let your child talk to you about their day, their worries, or their dreams. Ask open-ended questions to deepen the conversation, but avoid reacting emotionally or critically. The goal is to listen fully and show empathy.

💟 Heart Letters: Messages that Transform

Writing a weekly note and leaving it in a special place, such as your pillow or backpack, can be a powerful gesture to convey love and support. These short words are constant reminders of your presence and prayer in their lives.

Practical example: Write something simple but meaningful, such as, "*I'm here for you always. I love you and pray every day for your dreams and your protection.*" This small act lets them know that they are constantly loved and remembered.

Family Reset: Building Eternal Bonds

📖 Monthly Restoration Promise: Declaring God's Truth

Memorizing and proclaiming a Bible promise aloud for your child reinforces spiritual intercession and helps you keep the faith in challenging times. These divine words are pillars of strength for your children's lives.

Practical example: Choose a promise like Isaiah 49:25: *"I will save your children."* Repeat it daily and in times of prayer, declaring that this divine truth will be fulfilled in your lives. By doing this, you are sowing hope and trust in God's power.

⏳ One-on-One Time: Restoring Emotional Connection

Set aside at least one hour a week to spend one-on-one time with your child, without distractions like cell phones. These shared moments are opportunities to heal invisible cracks and build a stronger bond.

Practical example: Plan simple activities such as walking together, cooking, or simply chatting while sharing a coffee or snack. This exclusive time allows them to feel valued and heard.

Family Reset: Building Eternal Bonds

The Impact of Intercession on Your Children's Lives

Being an intercessory parent involves acting with intention to strengthen not only the emotional connection, but also the spiritual bond with your children. With tools like the intercessory notebook, the five-minute non-judgment, and one-on-one time, you can cultivate healthy relationships that reflect God's love. Prayer and constant love are the channel through which restoration and divine purpose are manifested in your lives.

Words of Hope: The Promise of Return

Prayer is the most powerful bond that binds a mother's heart to God, enabling her to intercede for her children even in the darkest of times. White also affirmed that through prayer, mothers can place their children in the arms of God.

No matter how far away your children may seem, there is a hope-filled divine promise: "*And your children shall return to their own land.*" (Jeremiah 31:17, RVR1960). This verse reminds us that there is always a frontier of return, an opportunity for God to work in their hearts and lead them back to the path of faith.

The Power of Persistent Prayer

Family Reset:Building Eternal Bonds

Distance, whether physical, emotional, or spiritual, is never a limit to God's power. When you cry out in faith and constancy, you are placing your children in the hands of the only one who can restore their lives and guide their steps back. That promise is clear: "*They will return.*"

Practical example: Take time daily to mention your children by name in prayer. He prays specifically for his protection, for his heart, and for his return to the Lord. Even if you don't see immediate changes, remember that each prayer is a seed that in time will bear fruit.

A promise that never fails

God assures us that His hand is not shortened to save nor His ear closed to hear. Trust that every prayer has power and that even though the path seems uncertain today, He is faithful to fulfill His promises. Do not stop praying, because in that intercession is the strength to sustain your family.

"Cry unto me, and I will answer thee, and teach thee great and hidden things which thou knowest not." (Jeremiah 33:3, RVR1960).

It's Never Too Late to Start: Restoring with Love and Purpose

Family Reset: Building Eternal Bonds

We can't go back to the past or undo mistakes or lost moments, but we have the power to start today, right here. A sincere word, a loving embrace, or a prayer lifted up to heaven can be the beginning of a restoration. It is in those simple gestures that the seeds of a new beginning are sown.

Your child doesn't need you to be perfect. He is not looking for an impeccable figure in you, but a heart willing to love, listen and be present. All he longs for is to know that your love remains, constant and sure, like the love of the father in the parable of the prodigal son. That love that waits unconditionally, with open arms and full of hope, ready to receive and embrace.

Heavenly Father's Example: Restoring Relationships with Grace

God shows us through the father of the prodigal son how to act when there is distance or wounds in a relationship:

- **Hope with hope:** The father never stopped believing in his son's return.
- **Receive with grace:** When your child returned, there were no reproaches, just a welcome hug.
- **Restore with love:** Instead of judging, the father celebrated the reunion and renewed their bond.

Family Reset: Building Eternal Bonds

"But the father said to his servants, 'Bring out the best garment, and clothe him; and put a ring on his hand, and shoes on his feet." (Luke 15:22, RVR1960).

The first step towards return

No matter how broken or distant the relationship may seem, there is always an opportunity to restore it. The important thing is to take the first step with humility and love. A kind word, a sincere hug, and fervent prayer can transform even the most hurting hearts.

Your child doesn't need perfection; He needs assurance of your unbreakable love. It is that love, a reflection of our heavenly Father's, that can restore and bring new life into the relationship.

Family Reset:Building Eternal Bonds

Family Reset: Building Eternal Bonds

Chapter 8: How to Forgive Without Losing Yourself

The Miracle of Reconciliation with Identity

There are wounds that are not seen, but are felt with every breath. Words that do not bleed, but they left scars on the soul. Betrayals that still hurt when remembered. In the family context, forgiveness is not a decorative option. It is **a spiritual and emotional urgency**.

But how do you forgive when the pain has been deep? How can we forgive without betraying our dignity? How to love again... without annulling what we are?

This chapter is a path to forgiveness that does not erase you, but **restores you without losing your essence**.

Forgiveness According to Heaven

God does not forgive superficially. He forgives from the blood, from the cross, from eternal love. He does not ask us to forget, but to surrender the right of revenge in order to receive **inner freedom.**

"For if you forgive men their trespasses, your heavenly Father will forgive you also." (Matthew 6:14)

Family Reset: Building Eternal Bonds

Forgiveness does not mean approval of sin. It is the act of freeing the soul from the poison of resentment.

To forgive is not to justify the unjustifiable. It is letting go of what binds you so that God will do justice in His own way... and you can live.

When forgiveness becomes an emotional prison

Camila wrote me a letter. He said: "They ask me to forgive, but I was the wounded one. Does it not matter what I suffered?"

Her father had humiliated her in childhood. His mother had been silent. Today, as an adult, she had a dysfunctional marriage... and a soul full of knots.

I replied with this phrase: "Forgiveness is not a betrayal of your pain. It is the medicine that your soul needs so as not to live enslaved to the past."

To forgive is not to allow more abuse. It is closing a wound with a scar... not with emotional pus.

What does it mean to forgive without getting lost?

1. It is to recognize the wound honestly. You cannot forgive what you deny.

Family Reset:Building Eternal Bonds

2. **It is deciding to heal, even if there are no apologies.** Forgiveness does not depend on the other. It's your leap of faith.
3. **It is to establish new limits.** You can forgive someone... and still put distance if necessary for your emotional or physical safety.
4. It is allowing the Holy Spirit to treat the wounded heart. He doesn't ignore your pain. He turns it into a testimony.
5. It is remembering that you were forgiven too. Not from perfection... but from grace.

Testimony: The Embrace That Broke 20 Years of Silence

David and his older brother had not spoken to each other since their father's death. An argument over inheritance separated them. Two decades of silence, reproaches, pride.

Until David became seriously ill. His wife, a faithful believer, said to him: "If you were to die today, with what accounts would you surrender your soul?"

He called his brother. It was not a long conversation. He just said, "I forgive you. And I ask your forgiveness." They both cried. Love returned. David lived five more years. His brother was the one who held him until his last breath.

Family Reset:Building Eternal Bonds
Tools for Practicing Family Forgiveness

💟 **Release letter**: Write down what you never said. Free yourself on paper. Then, if it's healthy and safe, share it. If not, burn it as a symbolic act.

🙏 **Prayer of Letting Go**: Every morning, say, "Lord, I give this wound to You. I don't want to carry her anymore."

🧱 **New boundary map**: Identify what you're willing to tolerate and what you won't accept anymore. Forgiveness should not erase your values.

📖 **Restoration Verse:** "Create in me, O God, a clean heart, and renew a right spirit within me." (Psalm 51:10)

🏠 **Family Forgiveness Ritual**: Once a month, as a family, share something you need to ask for or give forgiveness for. Close with prayer and hug.

The Healing Power of Forgiveness in the Home – Transforming the Home into a Sanctuary of Peace

Forgiveness is the balm that heals the deepest wounds of the human heart. In the context of the home, its power is even more transcendental. An unforgiven home becomes an emotional prison, where resentments and unhealed wounds imprison

Family Reset: Building Eternal Bonds

its inhabitants. Instead, a home where forgiveness reigns is transformed into a sanctuary, a space where God's grace flows freely and where relationships are restored and flourish.

Ellen G. White, in her work *The Christian Home*, states that where the Spirit of Christ dwells, there is humility, sweetness of character, and forgiveness.

These words remind us that forgiveness is not just a human act, but a manifestation of Christ's character in our lives. When we allow His spirit to dwell in our home, forgiveness becomes a natural and transformative practice.

Forgiveness in the Bible

The Bible offers us multiple teachings about forgiveness and its importance in our relationships. Some key verses include:

- **Ephesians 4:32**: "But be kind to one another, merciful, forgiving one another, just as God in Christ also forgave you." This verse calls us to imitate divine forgiveness in our daily interactions.
- **Colossians 3:13**: "Putting up with one another, and forgiving one another if anyone has a complaint against another; just as Christ forgave you, so do you." Here we are reminded that forgiveness is a reflection of Christ's love for us.

Family Reset: Building Eternal Bonds

- **Matthew 6:14-15**: "For if you forgive men their trespasses, your heavenly Father will also forgive you; but if you do not forgive men their trespasses, neither will your Father forgive you your trespasses." This passage underscores the connection between the forgiveness we give and the forgiveness we receive from God.

Forgiveness as Transformation

Forgiveness not only frees the giver, but also transforms the home environment. It is an act of humility and love that reflects the character of Christ and has the power to restore broken relationships. When we choose to forgive, we allow God's grace to work in our lives and in our families, creating a space where peace and harmony can flourish.

I once read in *The Adventist Home* that the home should be a place where love dwells—a love that flows like a still river, refreshing all within its reach.

This love, manifested through forgiveness, is what makes the home a sanctuary, a place where every member of the family can find refuge and restoration.

Reflection

Forgiveness is a divine tool that God has given us to heal and strengthen our relationships. In the home, its impact is especially powerful, transforming what could be an emotional prison into a space of freedom and love. This call to practice forgiveness is not just an invitation, but a sacred responsibility that reflects the character of Christ in our lives.

Conclusion: The Transformative Power of Forgiveness

Forgiving is not a sign of weakness; it is one of the greatest evidences that God dwells in our hearts. The act of forgiveness reflects the divine grace we have received and invites us to extend it to others. In a world where resentment and human justice often prevail, forgiveness is a countercultural act that liberates and transforms us.

The Bible teaches us that forgiveness is essential to our relationship with God and with others. In **Matthew 6:14-15**, Jesus declares, *"For if you forgive men their trespasses, your heavenly Father will also forgive you; but if you do not forgive men their trespasses, neither will your Father forgive you your trespasses."* This passage underscores that forgiveness not only benefits the other, but is also a requirement for fully experiencing God's grace.

When we forgive, we not only free the other from the burden of guilt, but we also free ourselves from the weight of resentment. **Ephesians 4:32** exhorts us, *"But be kind to one another, merciful, forgiving one another, just as God in Christ forgave you."* This call to mercy and forgiveness reminds us that we are

Family Reset:Building Eternal Bonds

recipients of divine grace and are therefore called to share it.

Ellen G. White, in her work *The Adventist Home*, we an learn that where the Spirit of Christ dwells, there is humility, sweetness of character, and forgiveness.

These words encapsulate the essence of forgiveness as a manifestation of Christ's character in our lives. When we choose to forgive, we allow His spirit to transform our home into a sanctuary of peace and love.

Today you can let go of that stone you've been carrying. You don't need to wear it anymore. Heaven begins when we stop demanding human justice and begin to live in divine grace. Forgiveness not only restores relationships, but it also frees us to live in the fullness of God's love.

Family Reset:Building Eternal Bonds

Chapter 9: Traditions that Heal, and Unite

Sowing Heaven Through Family Rituals

There are things that are not forgotten. The aroma of bread baked by grandma every Saturday, the prayers shared before bed, the songs sung on the way to school. These seemingly small details are actually the eternal threads that weave the family soul together. They are memories that not only remain in the memory, but also shape the character and strengthen the bonds between generations.

Family traditions are not mere customs. They are emotional anchors that connect us to our roots, spiritual refuges that remind us of God's presence in our daily lives, and invisible bridges that bind generations together with purpose and love. In a world where the fast pace threatens to uproot our deepest connections, traditions act as a balm that heals and binds.

The Bible reminds us of the importance of passing on values and teachings across generations. In **Deuteronomy 6:6-7**, we are instructed, *"And these words which I command you today shall be upon your heart; and you shall repeat them to your children, and you shall speak of them when you are at home, and walking in the way, and when you lie down, and when you get up."* This passage underscores how family rituals and traditions are vehicles for instilling faith and divine principles in the hearts of our children.

Family Reset:Building Eternal Bonds

A family without traditions is like a tree without roots: it can survive for a while, but it does not flourish or bear fruit. Traditions are the roots that anchor us in God's love and eternal purpose. The home should be a place where love dwells, a love that is manifested in kind words and deeds, a love that flows like a still river to refresh all who are within its reach. This love is cultivated and strengthened through traditions that reflect the values of heaven.

This chapter is an invitation to rescue, create, and strengthen traditions that heal, uplift, and connect. From family Bible reading to shared meals, every act can become a ritual that sows heaven on earth. Because when a family comes together around traditions that glorify God, not only memories are built, but also an eternal legacy.

God is a God of Living Memories
The power of the Rituals that connect Heaven and Earth

God, in his infinite wisdom, did not leave the human being without history or rituals that connect him with his presence. From the beginning, he established symbols and practices that act as living reminders of his faithfulness and love. The Sabbath, the Passover, the altar, the stones of the Jordan... each of these elements points to an eternal truth: *"Remember what I have done."*

Family Reset:Building Eternal Bonds

The Bible repeatedly calls us to preserve and pass on these living memories. In **Deuteronomy 6:6-9**, we are instructed, "And these words which I command you today shall be upon your heart; and you shall repeat them to your children, and you shall speak of them when you are at home, and when you walk by the way, and when you lie down, and when you get up. And you shall write them on the doorposts of your house, and on your gates." This mandate is not only an invitation to remember, but also to teach, to build a spiritual legacy that transcends generations.

We can emphasizes the importance of family rituals by stating: God has ordained that traditions be established in every family that uplift, ennoble, and strengthen. These traditions are not mere formalities; They are echoes of heaven on earth, practices that ennoble the soul and strengthen family ties.

When a family establishes holy and joyful rituals, such as home worship, joint prayer, or Sabbath celebration, it becomes a reflection of God's kingdom. These acts not only bind family members together, but they also anchor them in the hope and promise of redemption. **Psalm 78:4** reminds us: *"We will not hide them from his children, telling to the generation to come the praises of the Lord, and his power, and the wonders he has done."*

God is a God of living memories because He knows that the human heart needs tangible reminders of

Family Reset: Building Eternal Bonds

His grace. Every ritual, every tradition, is an opportunity to sow heaven on earth, to transform the everyday into something eternal. As White said time and time again, The home should be a place where love dwells, a love that flows like a still river to refresh all within reach.

This call to remember and to establish rituals is not only an invitation, but a sacred responsibility. But when a family lives within the framework of these living memories, it becomes a witness to God's transforming power, a beacon of light in a world in desperate need of hope.

Traditions that harm, vs. traditions that heal, The Transformative Power of Family Traditions

Not all traditions are healthy. Some are empty cultural burdens that perpetuate harmful patterns, such as emotional violence, machismo, or graceless religiosity. These traditions, far from building, erode family ties and distort God's purpose for our lives. However, true healing traditions have the power to transform, uplift, and connect families to God and to each other.

The traditions that heal

Family Reset:Building Eternal Bonds

Healing traditions are those that reflect the values of heaven and serve an eternal purpose. Here are some traditions:

- **They connect us to God**: They act as living reminders of his love and faithfulness. In **Deuteronomy 6:6-7,** we are instructed, "And these words which I command you today shall be upon your heart; and you shall repeat them to your children, and you shall speak of them when you are at home, and walking in the way, and when you lie down, and when you get up." This passage underscores the importance of transmitting the faith through family practices.
- **They reinforce family identity**: They help family members understand who they are and what their purpose is in God's plan. **Psalm 78:4** reminds us: *"We will not hide them from his children, telling to the generation to come the praises of the Lord, and his power, and the wonders he has done."*
- **Help children feel part of something sacred**: Family rituals, such as prayer together or reading the Bible, teach them that they are part of a larger divine story.
- **They rewrite history when we come from broken contexts**: Healing traditions have the power to redeem and restore, offering a fresh start based on the principles of love and grace.

Family Reset: Building Eternal Bonds

God has ordained that traditions be established in every family that uplift, ennoble, and strengthen. These words remind us that traditions are not just human practices, but divine tools for building homes that reflect God's character.

Reflection

Healing traditions are a gift from God to families. When established with purpose and love, they become deep roots that support the tree of family life. In contrast, harmful traditions must be evaluated and, if necessary, replaced by practices that glorify God and strengthen family bonds.

This call to discern between traditions that harm and traditions that heal is not only an invitation, but a sacred responsibility. Because when a family lives within the framework of healing traditions, it becomes a living witness to God's transforming power.

Testimony: When a Sabbath Changed History

Mauro's family came from three generations without faith. He was introduced to the gospel at age 27. His wife resisted. Her children grew up between screens and sarcasm.

Family Reset: Building Eternal Bonds

One day, Mauro decided to start with a tradition: Every Saturday, at dawn, he would prepare breakfast, read a verse and give thanks together. Just that.

At first, it was difficult. Then, they waited for Saturday. Afterwards, the children asked for prayer. A year later, the whole family was baptized.

"A little tradition can ignite a flame that spans generations." (Mauro told me, with tears in his eyes.)

How to create family traditions that unite and uplift?

🌿 **Saturday, family of gratitude.** Every Saturday at sunset, share 3 things you are grateful for and say a prayer of praise together.

📖 **Verse of the week.** Write a Bible text on a blackboard or on the refrigerator. Read it and comment on it during the week.

🎵 **Song of blessing.** Choose a praise song as a "family hymn." Sing it on birthdays, achievements, farewells or difficult moments.

🍲 **Inheritance recipe.** Cook a recipe from grandma or the country of origin together. As you cook, tell family stories.

Family Reset:Building Eternal Bonds

♥ **Letter of the month.** Once a month, each member writes a short letter to another family member. They are exchanged at a special dinner.

Day of service. Once a quarter, choose an activity to serve together: visit an elder, cook for a neighbor, clean up a park.

Spiritual Traditions That Transform
Shaping Character and Preparing for Heaven

Spiritual traditions are at the heart of true homeschooling. They are the habits, words, and customs that are repeated every day that have the power to shape character, set priorities, and prepare children to be citizens of heaven. White, in her work *Education*, states that true education begins in the home with the habits, the words, the customs that are repeated every day. These words remind us that traditions are not mere cultural practices, but divine tools for forming lives that reflect the character of Christ.

The Impact of Spiritual Traditions

Spiritual traditions have a profound impact on children's lives and family dynamics. Here are some possible traditions:

- **Shape character:** Through the repetition of holy habits, such as family prayer, Bible reading, and joint worship, children learn values that guide

Family Reset: Building Eternal Bonds

them in their relationship with God and others. **Proverbs 22:6** instructs us, "*Train up a child in his way, and when he is old he will not depart from it.*"

- **They set priorities**: Spiritual traditions teach children to put God at the center of their lives, helping them discern what is truly important.
- **Prepare for Heaven**: Every spiritual tradition is an opportunity to sow seeds of faith and hope in the hearts of children, preparing them to live as citizens of God's kingdom.

Ellen G. White emphasizes the importance of spiritual traditions in character formation and preparation for eternal life. In *The Christian Home*, we can read the God has ordained that traditions be established in every family that uplift, ennoble, and strengthen. Not only do these traditions strengthen family bonds, but they also act as a bridge between heaven and earth.

Reflection

Transformative spiritual traditions are a divine gift to families. When established with purpose and love, they have the power to shape lives, strengthen relationships, and prepare children to fulfill their eternal purpose. This call to establish spiritual traditions is not just an invitation, but a sacred responsibility that reflects God's character in our lives.

Family Reset:Building Eternal Bonds
Conclusion: The Power of Family Traditions

A family tradition doesn't need to be expensive or elaborate; Her true value lies in her intention, perseverance and the love that inspires her. Traditions are not simply empty rituals, but opportunities to create sacred memories that transcend time and strengthen family bonds. They are the bricks with which a spiritual heritage is built that does not fade.

The Bible reminds us of the importance of establishing practices that reflect God's love and grace. In **Deuteronomy 6:6-7**, we are instructed, *"And these words which I command you today shall be upon your heart; and you shall repeat them to your children, and you shall speak of them when you are at home, and walking in the way, and when you lie down, and when you get up."* This passage underscores that family traditions are a means of transmitting faith and divine values to future generations.

God has ordained that traditions be established in every family that uplift, ennoble, and strengthen. These words invite us to create traditions that not only connect family members to one another, but also unite them to God.

Today you have the opportunity to start a new story. A tradition, no matter how simple, can become the first brick of an eternal legacy. Whether it's a shared

Family Reset:Building Eternal Bonds

prayer at the end of the day, a family meal, or a moment of reflection on the Sabbath, every intentional act has the power to sow heaven on earth.

Family traditions are more than memories; they are a living testimony of God's love in action. By building them with purpose and love, you are leaving a legacy that will not only impact your family, but also glorify God.

Family Reset:Building Eternal Bonds

Family Reset:Building Eternal Bonds

Chapter 10: The Joy of Being a Purposeful Family

When Living Together Becomes Shared Mission

Many families live under the same roof, but without a shared direction. They fulfill routines, celebrate dates and support each other in problems, but they do not know why they are together or where they are going. Living as a family without purpose is like navigating without a compass: you move forward, but without direction. However, when a family discovers its divine calling, everything is transformed into joy. Everyday tasks, difficult trials, achievements, and even losses take on eternal meaning.

God's Purpose for the Family

The Bible teaches us that the family is not a human creation, but a divine design with an eternal purpose. In **Joshua 24:15**, it is declared: "*But I and my house will serve Jehovah.*" This verse reflects the call of every family to live in service and worship to God. When a family embraces this purpose, its members find unity and direction in their shared mission.

God created the family as a space to teach, love, and reflect His character. In **Deuteronomy 6:6-7**, we are instructed, "And these words which I command you today shall be upon your heart; and you shall repeat them to your children, and you shall speak of them

Family Reset:Building Eternal Bonds

when you are at home, and walking in the way, and when you lie down, and when you get up." This passage underscores the importance of passing on faith and divine values through generations.

Ellen G. White, in her work The Christian Home, writes: The home should be a place where love dwells, a love that flows like a still river to refresh all who are within its reach. These words remind us that the purpose of the family is not only to survive, but to thrive in love and unity, reflecting the character of Christ in every interaction.

Transforming the home into a space of joy

When a family lives with purpose, every aspect of life is transformed. Everyday tasks become opportunities to serve God, difficult trials are seen as tools to grow in faith, and accomplishments are celebrated as divine blessings. Even losses can be faced with hope, knowing that God has an eternal plan for each member of the family.

Reflection

This chapter is an invitation for your family to not only survive, but to live with eternal purpose. Discovering the divine call for your home is the first step in transforming routine into mission, effort into joy, and fellowship into a reflection of heaven on earth. Because when a family lives with purpose, they find not only direction, but also the joy of knowing that they are fulfilling God's plan.

Family Reset: Building Eternal Bonds

God calls families, not just individuals

When God decided to change the world, He didn't call an army first... he called a family: **Abraham, Sarah, Isaac.**

"In thy seed shall all the nations of the earth be blessed, because thou hast obeyed my voice." (Genesis 22:18)

Every family is to be a missionary agency from heaven on earth.

It doesn't matter if your family is large or small, if you have children or live alone with your husband. **God has a mission for you.**

Testimony: A family that found its calling. The Solis family was common. They worked, studied, attended church. But something was missing. One day, at a family camp, they heard a phrase that changed their lives: **"A family without a mission is a house without a soul."**

From that day on they began to pray, "Lord, what purpose do you have for us?"

The answer came: every Sunday, they would prepare food and devotionals for the homeless. What started with 3 bags, became a chain of help. Today, that family has reached hundreds of lives.

Family Reset:Building Eternal Bonds

They did not change jobs. They did not go on missionaries. They only **turned their home into an instrument of heaven.**

How to discover the purpose of our family?

A Call to Live with Intention and Mission

God has a unique purpose for every family, a special calling that aligns with the gifts, passions, and experiences He has already placed in us. Discovering this purpose not only transforms family life, but also enables us to be instruments of his love and grace in the world. Here are practical steps to find that eternal purpose:

1. Ask yourself: What gifts and passions unite us?

Hospitality? Music? Prayer? Service? Education? God does not call us to what we cannot do; He uses what He has already put into us. Every talent and passion is a tool that can be used for your glory. **1 Peter 4:10** reminds us: *"Let each one minister it to others according to the gift he has received, as good stewards of the manifold grace of God."*

2. Ask God in Prayer

Prayer is the first step in aligning our plans with God's. Entrusting our works to the Lord gives us clarity and direction. As **Proverbs 16:3 says**: *"Commit your works to the Lord, and your thoughts will*

Family Reset:Building Eternal Bonds

be established." Through prayer, God reveals His purpose and gives us the wisdom to walk in His will.

3. Ask the world: Which need hurts us the most?

Mission is born of love that hurts. That which moves us deeply can be a sign of the place where God is calling us to serve. **Matthew 25:40** reminds us, *"Truly I say to you, inasmuch as you did it to one of the least of these my brethren, you did it to me."* Identifying the needs around us helps us find our place in God's plan.

4. Look for small opportunities

Don't expect a big stage to start. Purpose begins with simple, consistent, and sincere steps. In a Christian Home, every family is to be a missionary agency from heaven on earth. Small daily actions, such as helping a neighbor, praying together as a family, or teaching children to serve, are the building blocks of an eternal legacy.

Reflection
Discovering our family's purpose is a journey of faith, love, and obedience. It doesn't matter if your family is large or small, if you have children or live alone with your husband or wife. God has a mission

Family Reset: Building Eternal Bonds

for you, a mission that can transform not only your home, but also the world around you. Today is the day to begin to walk in that eternal purpose.

Tools to build a family with a mission

🌐 **Family slogan.** Create a phrase that expresses your calling. Example: "We love, we serve, we pray together."

📅 **Impact calendar.** Choose one solidarity or spiritual action per month: visiting, serving, writing, praying for others.

📖 **Family Missionary Book.** Keep a record of what you have done, what God has done, and what you dream of doing.

🙏 **Worship with a purpose.** Once a week, pray specifically for the calling God gave you as a family.

💬 **Network of gratitude.** Motivate each other by remembering the good you have lived together in service.

Purpose brings joy... even in the test
   Strength and Unity in Difficult Times

It is no coincidence that families with a mission survive crises better. When the purpose is clear, pain

Family Reset:Building Eternal Bonds

does not destroy, but strengthens. Trials, far from being insurmountable obstacles, become opportunities to grow in faith, love, and unity. In a purpose-driven home, differences diminish, love comes into focus, and shared mission becomes the anchor that sustains the family through storms.

Purpose in the Bible

The Bible teaches us that divine purpose gives meaning and direction, even in the most difficult of times. In **Romans 8:28**, we are assured, *"And we know that all things work together for good to those who love God, to those who are the called according to His purpose."* This verse reminds us that when we live in God's purpose, even trials work for our good and strengthen our faith.

Furthermore, **Isaiah 41:10** encourages us: "Do not be afraid, for I am with you; do not be dismayed, for I am your God who makes you strong; I will always help you, I will always uphold you with the right hand of my righteousness." This passage underscores that, in the midst of difficulties, God is present to sustain and guide us.

Famiy Purpose

The families that work together for others grow more united with one another. These words reflect the truth that when a family unites around a common cause, trials not only strengthen their mission but also their bonds. Service to others not

Family Reset: Building Eternal Bonds

only benefits those who are helped, but it also transforms and unites those who offer it.

Reflection

Purpose brings joy even in trial, because it gives us a reason to persevere and a hope that transcends circumstances. Families with a mission don't just survive crises; they thrive in them, finding strength in their unity and direction in their divine calling. Today is the day to embrace that purpose and allow it to transform your home into a haven of love, faith, and hope.

Conclusion

The Healing Power of Forgiveness in the Home
Transforming the Home into a Sanctuary of Peace

Forgiveness is the foundation on which homes filled with love, peace, and unity are built. Without forgiveness, a home can become an emotional prison, where resentments and unhealed wounds imprison its inhabitants. But when forgiveness reigns, the home is transformed into a sanctuary, a place where God's grace flows freely and where relationships are restored and flourish.

Where the spirit of Christ dwells, there is humility, there is sweetness of character, there is forgiveness.

Family Reset:Building Eternal Bonds

These words remind us that forgiveness is not just a human act, but a manifestation of Christ's character in our lives. When we allow His spirit to dwell in our home, forgiveness becomes a natural and transformative practice.

Forgiveness in the Bible

The Bible offers us multiple teachings about forgiveness and its importance in our relationships. Some key verses include:

- **Ephesians 4:32 (RVR1960):** *"But be kind to one another, merciful, forgiving one another, just as God also forgave you in Christ."* This verse calls us to imitate divine forgiveness in our daily interactions.
- **Colossians 3:13 (RVR1960):** "Bearing with one another, and forgiving one another if anyone has a complaint against another; just as Christ forgave you, so do you." Here we are reminded that forgiveness is a reflection of Christ's love for us.
- **Matthew 6:14-15 (RVR1960):** "For if you forgive men their trespasses, your heavenly Father will also forgive you; but if you do not forgive men their trespasses, neither will your Father forgive you your trespasses." This passage underscores the connection between the forgiveness we give and the forgiveness we receive from God.

Forgiveness as transformation

Family Reset:Building Eternal Bonds

Forgiveness not only frees the giver, but also transforms the home environment. It is an act of humility and love that reflects the character of Christ and has the power to restore broken relationships. When we choose to forgive, we allow God's grace to work in our lives and in our families, creating a space where peace and harmony can flourish.

The home should be a place where love dwells, a love that flows like a still river to refresh all within reach. This love, manifested through forgiveness, is what makes the home a sanctuary, a place where every member of the family can find refuge and restoration.

Final Thoughts

Forgiveness is a divine tool that God has given us to heal and strengthen our relationships. In the home, its impact is especially powerful, transforming what could be an emotional prison into a space of freedom and love. This call to practice forgiveness is not just an invitation, but a sacred responsibility that reflects the character of Christ in our lives.

Family Reset: Building Eternal Bonds

Chapter 11: From Ruins to Redemption

Your home can be a piece of heaven

If you've made it this far, it's not by chance. Something in your soul longs for more than clean walls and a tidy life. You long for a heaven at home. A family where love is not forced, where forgiveness flows, where prayers are not extinguished, where bonds withstand storms, where purpose is dreamed of, and where Jesus is an inhabitant, not a visitor.

The Divine Design for the Home

From the beginning, God designed the family as the first sanctuary, a place where His presence could dwell and where human bonds reflected His eternal love. In **Joshua 24:15**, we are reminded: *"But I and my household will serve the Lord."* This commitment is not only a declaration of faith, but an invitation to turn the home into a space where heaven is anticipated on earth.

The home should be a place where love dwells, a love that flows like a still river to refresh all who are within its reach. These words invite us to transform our homes into havens of peace, love, and hope, where every member of the family can find comfort and purpose.

Family Reset: Building Eternal Bonds

Lessons from the trip

On this journey we have walked together through wounds, hopes, decisions and restorations. We have recalled that:

- **The family was the first sanctuary**: A place where God dwells and where His love is manifested.
- **Time is the seed of the eternal**: Every moment invested in the family has an eternal impact.
- **Love heals what words broke**: Grace and forgiveness have the power to restore what seemed lost.
- **Prayer transforms the spiritual climate**: Raising our voices to God changes not only our circumstances, but also our hearts.
- **Family purpose gives soul to the home**: Living with intention and mission unites the family in a divine calling.

Reflection

And now it's your turn. You don't need a perfect family to have a heavenly home. You just need a willing heart, a burning faith, and a sincere prayer that says, *"Lord, start with me. Make my home an anticipated heaven."*

For heaven begins where there are eternal bonds, where God's love is the foundation, and where each member of the family becomes a reflection of his grace. Today is the day to transform your home into

Family Reset:Building Eternal Bonds

a piece of heaven, a place where redemption is not only expected, but lived.

Tools to build a heavenly home

Adapted for each family stage

These resources are simple, but if you use them consistently, they can transform the spiritual environment of your home. Every practice, verse, and tradition is designed to strengthen family bonds and bring your family closer to God's purpose.

📖 Verses for the Family Heart

The following verses are spiritual pillars that can guide and strengthen your family:

- **Psalm 127:1**: "Unless the Lord builds the house, those who build it labor in vain; if the Lord does not guard the city, he keeps watch in vain."
- **Isaiah 49:25**: "For I will contend with him that contends with you, and I will save your children."
- **Proverbs 15:1**: "A gentle answer takes away anger; but the harsh word makes anger rise."
- **Proverbs 22:6**: "Train up a child in his way, and when he is old he will not depart from it."
- **Joshua 24:15**: "But I and my household will serve the Lord."

Family Reset: Building Eternal Bonds

Family Spiritual Exercises

Establishing daily spiritual practices can transform the emotional and spiritual climate of your home. Here's a weekly guide:

Day	Spiritual Activity	Estimated Time
Monday	Prayer of gratitude as a couple	5 min
Tuesday	Family Bible Reading	10 min
Wednesday	Individual Silent Prayer	5 min
Thursday	Share Blessings of the Week	10 min
Friday	Family worship with music	20 min
Saturday	Day of Service to Someone Else	Variable

Family Reset: Building Eternal Bonds

Day	Spiritual Activity	Estimated Time
Sunday	Spiritual Goals Review	15 min

Phrases that heal the home environment

Words have the power to build or destroy. Use these phrases to strengthen family bonds:

- "I hear you."
- "What can I help you with today?"
- "Thank you for being here."
- "Sorry if I hurt you."
- "I'm proud of you."
- "I prayed for you today."
- "You are a gift from God to me."

Family Tradition Ideas

Family traditions are powerful tools for creating eternal bonds and strengthening faith:

- **Testimony Night**: Once a month, share all that God has worked in your lives.
- **Breakfast with a purpose**: On the first Sunday of each month, we read a Bible promise together.

Family Reset:Building Eternal Bonds

- **Affirmation Circle**: On birthdays or milestones, each member shares something positive about the honoree.
- **Answered Prayer Box**: Keep notes with divine answers and read them together at the end of the year.

Final Thoughts

God has ordained that traditions be established in every family that uplift, ennoble, and strengthen. These words remind us that every spiritual practice and every family tradition has the power to transform the home into a reflection of heaven.

Today you can start implementing these resources in your home. You don't need perfection, just perseverance and a willing heart. Because heaven begins where there is love, purpose, and eternal bonds.

Family Reset:Building Eternal Bonds
Meet the Author

Dr. Mariangeli Morauske is an exceptional figure whose multifaceted trajectory spans academia, leadership, and spiritual guidance. Her tireless dedication to education and service has led to significant contributions in roles such as teacher, principal, dean, scholar, and chaplain.

As an educator, Dr. Morauske has transformed the lives of countless students by inspiring them with her passion for knowledge and commitment to excellence. His innovative pedagogical approaches, combined with his in-depth knowledge of his field, have earned him the respect and admiration of both colleagues and students.

In the spiritual realm, Dr. Morauske serves as a chaplain, offering emotional support and spiritual guidance with compassion and unwavering faith. Her dedication has brought comfort and hope to those facing challenges, leaving a deep mark on their lives.

In her personal life, Dr. Morauske exemplifies harmony and strength. She is a devoted wife to her husband, Daniel Morauske, and a loving mother to their two children: Leilani, a registered nurse and clinical educator at a hospital on the Navajo Indian

Family Reset:Building Eternal Bonds

Reservation in Arizona, and Josiah, an information technology specialist based in Fort Worth, Texas. His ability to balance professional and family responsibilities is a testament to his exceptional character.

Dr. Morauske has a diverse academic background, including a master's degree in Counseling Psychology from National University, a master's degree in pastoral ministry from Andrews University, and a doctorate in medicine. This strong academic foundation reflects their comprehensive commitment to physical, mental, and spiritual well-being.

Her life trajectory has led her to reside in Israel, Puerto Rico, Venezuela, Colombia and Mexico, before settling in Alvarado, Texas. These global experiences have enriched his perspective and allowed him to develop a deep understanding of different cultures and communities.

Above all, Dr. Morauske defines herself as a servant of God, dedicated to living a life of faith, purpose, and service. Her personal story is a testament to the strength of love, perseverance, and the positive impact her commitment inspires in others.

Family Reset:Building Eternal Bonds
My Notes

Family Reset:Building Eternal Bonds
My Notes

Family Reset:Building Eternal Bonds
My Notes

Family Reset:Building Eternal Bonds
My Notes

Family Reset: Building Eternal Bonds
My Notes

Family Reset:Building Eternal Bonds
My Notes

Family Reset:Building Eternal Bonds
Bibliography

Balswick, J. O., & Balswick, J. K. (2007). *The Family: A Christian Perspective on the Contemporary Home*. Grand Rapids, MI: Baker Academic.

King James Version Bible (KJV). (1611). *King James Bible*. Thomas Nelson Publishers.

Bounds, E. M. (1990). *The Complete Works of E.M. Bounds on Prayer*. Grand Rapids, MI: Baker Books.

Chapman, G. (1992). *The Five Love Languages*. Chicago, IL: Northfield Publishing.

Chapman, G. (1992). The Five Love Languages: How to Express Heartfelt Commitment to Your Mate. Northfield Publishing.

Chapman, G. (2007). Everybody Wins: The Chapman Guide to Solving Conflicts Without Arguing. Carol Stream, IL: Tyndale House.

Chapman, G. (2010). *The Five Love Languages*. Chicago, IL: Northfield Publishing.

Chapman, G. (2012). *The 5 Love Languages of Teenagers*. Chicago, IL: Northfield Publishing.

Chapman, G. (2014). *The 5 Love Languages of Children*. Chicago, IL: Northfield Publishing.

Family Reset:Building Eternal Bonds

Clinton, T., & Sibcy, G. (2006). *Why You Do the Things You Do: The Secret to Healthy Relationships*. Nashville, TN: Thomas Nelson.

Cloud, H., & Townsend, J. (2001). *Boundaries: When to Say Yes, How to Say No*. Grand Rapids, MI: Zondervan.

Cloud, H., & Townsend, J. (2006). *Boundaries with Kids: When to Say Yes, When to Say No*. Grand Rapids, MI: Zondervan.

Covey, S. R. (1989). *The 7 Habits of Highly Effective Families*. New York, NY: Simon & Schuster.

Dobson, J. (2005). *Facing the challenges of parenting*. Carol Stream, IL: Tyndale House Publishers.

Dobson, J. (2010). *Bringing Up Girls*. Carol Stream, IL: Tyndale House Publishers.

Doherty, W. J. (1997). The Intentional Family: Simple Rituals to Strengthen Family Ties. New York, NY: Avon Books.

Enright, R. D. (2015). Forgiveness Is a Choice: A Step-by-Step Process for Resolving Anger and Restoring Hope. Washington, DC: APA LifeTools.

Fiese, B. H. (2006). *Family Routines and Rituals*. New Haven, CT: Yale University Press.

Family Reset:Building Eternal Bonds

Gottman, J. M., & Silver, N. (1999). *The Seven Principles for Making Marriage Work*. New York, NY: Three Rivers Press.

Gottman, J. M., & Silver, N. (1999). *The Seven Principles for Making Marriage Work*. New York, NY: Three Rivers Press.

Lewis, C. S. (1960). *The Weight of Glory*. New York, NY: HarperOne.

Lucado, M. (2003). *Face your giants*. Nashville, TN: Nelson Group.

Rosberg, G., & Rosberg, B. (2003). *How to improve communication in your marriage*. Little Rock, AR: Family Life.

Satir, V. (1983). *Peoplemaking*. Palo Alto, CA: Science and Behavior Books.

Stanley, C. (2010). *How to Reach Your Full Potential for God*. Nashville, TN: Thomas Nelson.

Stanley, C. (2012). *The Power of Prayer in a Believer's Life*. Grand Rapids, MI: Chosen Books.

Townsend, J., & Cloud, H. (2002). *How People Grow: What the Bible Reveals About Personal Growth*. Grand Rapids, MI: Zondervan.

Warren, R. (2002). *A life with purpose*. Grand Rapids, MI: Vida Publishers.

Family Reset:Building Eternal Bonds

White, E. G. (1892). *The Way to Christ*. Mountain View, CA: Pacific Press Publishing Association.

White, E. G. (1893). *Fundamentals of Christian Education*. Nashville, TN: Southern Publishing Association.

White, E. G. (1898). *The Desire of Ages*. Mountain View, CA: Pacific Press Publishing Association.

White, E. G. (1903). *Education*. Mountain View, CA: Pacific Press Publishing Association.

White, E. G. (1905). *The Ministry of Healing*. Mountain View, CA: Pacific Press Publishing Association.

White, E. G. (1905). *The Ministry of Kindness*. Mountain View, CA: Pacific Press Publishing Association.

White, E. G. (1952). *The Christian Home*. Mountain View, CA: Pacific Press Publishing Association.

White, E. G. (1957). *Counsel for the Church*. Buenos Aires: Asociación Casa Editora Sudamericana.

Valenzuela, A. (2010). Transforma tu familia a través de la renovación del entendimiento. [Libro fuera de producción].

Valenzuela, A. (2003). *Casados pero contestos*. [Libro fuera de producción].

Family Reset:Building Eternal Bonds

Valenzuela, A. (2008). *Casados pero contestos*. [Libro fuera de producción].

Valenzuela, A. (2005). *Como Fortalezer la Familia.* [Libro fuera de producción].

www.ingramcontent.com/pod-product-compliance
Lightning Source LLC
Chambersburg PA
CBHW031710230426
43668CB00006B/178